The MYTHOLOGY
of VOICE

Darsie Bowden

Series Editor,
Charles I. Schuster

Boynton/Cook Publishers
HEINEMANN
Portsmouth, NH

Boynton/Cook Publishers, Inc.
A subsidiary of Reed Elsevier Inc.
361 Hanover Street
Portsmouth, NH 03801–3912
http://www.boyntoncook.com

Offices and agents throughout the world

Library of Congress Cataloging-in-Publication Data
Bowden, Darsie.
    Mythology of voice / by Darsie Bowden.
      p. cm. — (CrossCurrents)
    Includes bibliographical references.
    ISBN 0-86709-481-8
    1. English language—Rhetoric—Study and teaching. 2. Report writing—Study
and teaching (Higher). 3. Report writing—Study and teaching (Secondary).
4. English language—Composition and exercises. 5. Rhetoric—Psychological
aspects. 6. Individuality. I. Title. II. Series: CrossCurrents (Portsmouth, N.H.)
PE1404.B67 1999
808'.042'07—dc21   99-34080
                                                                CIP

Consulting Editor: Charles I. Schuster
Production: Abigail M. Heim
Cover design: Darci Mehall, Aureo Design
Manufacturing: Louise Richardson

Printed in the United States of America on acid-free paper
03 02 01 00 99 DA 1 2 3 4 5

Contents

Contents

Acknowledgments

As with most books, this could not have been completed without the generous support and contributions of a great many people. Foremost among them is Charles Schuster who, as editor of this series, gave me the time and encouragement I needed to complete the project I wanted. I am also indebted to W. Ross Winterowd, who promoted this project from the outset and has had enormous influence—even though he may not agree to the uses to which I have put it—and to Leo Braudy, Edward Finegan, Donald Freeman, and especially James P. Gee for their discerning questions and comments and their valuable advice on early drafts. My colleagues at DePaul University, David Jolliffe, Gerald Mulderig, Lucy Rinehart, and William Gartner (who furnished technical expertise), were extraordinarily generous with their time and suggestions. DePaul University provided significant financial support in the form of two summer research grants and a paid leave of absence. Thanks also to Ellen Alperstein, Debbie Martinson, Mark Shadle, Sam Greeley, and John Holland, who all provided valuable feedback, and to family and friends for putting up with what must at times have seemed like utter nonsense.

Introduction

Voice is a metaphor that is richly provocative. It is difficult to define, difficult to know how to use in one's writing, and difficult to analyze and explain in the writing of others. It has been used increasingly by marginalized groups as a metaphor of power, tying power in some way to an aural dimension. Voice as a concept has fueled a sizeable body of work in literary studies and narratology in an effort to identify the speaker or to disentangle speaker(s) from author. And it has informed countless studies and debates (some of them empirical, some of them contemplative, some of them caustically argumentative) in composition and rhetoric. Peter Elbow, one of the most enthusiastic voice proponents, wrote in 1981 that voice "is what most people have in their speech but lack in their writing—namely, a sound or texture—the sound of 'them'" (288). What that texture is, or what people "sound like" when they write, is a conceptual problem readily acknowledged by voice advocates. The difficulty in being precise about voice is also the reason why powerful writing is so troublesome to produce. With unfortunate circularity, Elbow has argued that "real voice" can be identified when readers feel a "resonance" not necessarily with the writer, but with "the words and themselves" (300). To find their writing voice, writers have to work at it—there are numerous techniques designed to help—until voice happens.

But this is only one way that voice has been considered. In fact—and what makes voice such an interesting and controversial term—the permutations and varying conceptions of voice, especially during the 1970s and 1980s, make voice difficult to completely support or to completely reject as a useful metaphor for textual analysis or for pedagogy. Even in the 1990s, an era of pluralized or multiple voices, while deftly avoiding the concept of a single authentic writing voice, theorists haven't been able to relinquish it in favor of other metaphors. Rather, they hasten to reconceive it to accommodate a different pedagogical paradigm. For example, in her textbook *Work in Progress*, Lisa Ede writes:

> Just as you dress differently on different occasions, as a writer you assume different voices in different situations. If you're writing an essay about a personal experience, you may work hard to create a strong personal voice in your essay. . . . If you're writing a report or essay exam, you will adopt a more formal, public tone. Whatever the situation, the

choices you make as you write and revise . . . will determine how readers interpret and respond to your presence in the text. (1989, 158)

However it is framed, voice is a pivotal metaphor in composition
and rhetoric studies because it focuses attention on authorship, on
identity, on narrative, and on power. As might be expected then, discussions of voice are often polarizing because the issues themselves are
highly controversial. The concept of voice in writing, for example, links
oral language with written, even while theorists debate over distinctions between speech and writing, oral and literate societies, and spoken language and written language in the classroom. Furthermore, the
notion of "authentic voice," the buzzword of the voice proponents of
the late 1960s and early 1970s, raises the issue of an authentic, unitary
self versus a mutable, social self (or selves) that pits "traditionalists"
against postmodernists.

In this book, I will argue that voice has served an important function in the movement away from current-traditional rhetoric, but
that, as a metaphor, it has outlived its usefulness. I will show how
voice epitomizes a logocentric, Eurocentric, patriarchal approach to discourse that—despite the fact that both literary theory and composition theory have embraced multiculturalism, electronic technology and
feminism—remains stubbornly embedded in our conversations about
texts. Underlying my argument is the assumption that there can be no
such thing as voice, that it was a metaphor of particular historical moment, and that that moment has passed. The last two chapters suggest
metaphors that may be more productive in talk about texts and what
texts do.

Why pay so much attention to the metaphors we use? It has become a commonly accepted belief that language shapes, to a significant
degree, the ways we view reality. Since much if not all of language is
arguably metaphorical, metaphors can be extraordinarily powerful in
conditioning what we say, do, and understand, and how we teach and
learn. Many of the metaphors we use are so embedded in everyday usage that we are unaware we are using them; consequently, they remain
largely unexamined. As with many things that are used uncritically,
metaphors can be quite dangerous in that they perpetuate the privileging of certain views of reality and the devaluation of others. Voice is one
such metaphor.

For the purpose of demonstrating and explaining how entrenched
voice is in the Western psyche, I look at a broad spectrum of antece-
dents from Plato's well-known discussion of writing to postmodern critique of phonocentrism. I use examples from both literary criticism and
composition theory to show when, how, and why voice gained popularity in the late 1960s, and, in so doing, I hope to expose the underly-

ing assumptions that make voice a liability rather than an effective "critical tool" (Elbow) in our talk about texts and rhetorical strategies.

This book can be rightly criticized for having tackled both too much and too little, for making assertions that have been made before and for making other statements that are controversial and disputable. My primary goal for this book is to raise questions and propose responses about the viability of the voice metaphor, using the history of composition and rhetoric as a backdrop. If this study can do that, then I have been successful.

Chapter One

The Voice in Literature

When stories came to be written, narrators retained (though not inevitably) strong personal marks—referring to themselves as "I"; offering judgments, opinions, generalizations; describing their own persons or habitats, and the like. The term "voice" was naturally, if figuratively, transferred to represent the means by which those activities occurred. It is a metaphor that continues to be widely used but insufficiently examined by narratology. . . . [N]o one to my knowledge has asked whether it really clarifies what it is supposed to name.
(Seymour Chatman, *Coming to Terms*, 118)

The disciplines of composition studies and literary studies have always been closely tied—historically, politically, and philosophically. For good or for ill, trends in literary criticism, including New Criticism, modernism, postmodernism, reader-response theory, and poststructuralism have had profound influence on how composition theorists, teachers, and students deal with and talk about writing. In fact, the two disciplines are at many points so intertwined that one might be hard pressed to articulate precise disciplinary boundaries. While it is not my purpose here to evaluate the merits or drawbacks of these interconnections, a considerable amount can be learned about voice as it has been used in literary studies. Voice was used by literary critics years before it became a staple in composition journals, textbooks, and classrooms; moreover our understanding of voice is strongly conditioned by how it has been used in literary theory, particularly narratology. To illustrate both the appeal and limitations of voice, and to help elucidate some of the underlying assumptions that are central to how voice is perceived and used in composition, this opening chapter explores how voice functions in literary narratives.

Let's begin with an example from Margaret Atwood, who opens her novel *Bodily Harm* with the following sentence: "This is how I got here, says Rennie." (1989, 11) After a line break, the first-person narrative explains: "It was the day after Jake left. I walked back to the house around five. I'd been over at the market and I was carrying the shopping basket as well as my purse." In these early sentences, Atwood sets up a narrative framework in which the main character, Rennie, lays out her situation, "saying" or telling her story to an anonymous narrator (and, of course, to the reader). The reader is given no indication as to whom Rennie is speaking or to what occasioned the narrative. After four pages, there is a physical break marked by white space, at which point the narrative switches to the third-person singular; the telling of Rennie's story is no longer in her own words, or at least this is what a reader is given to assume. The narrator, however, seems to be the same, but now the audience—through the third-person narrative—is privy as much to what Rennie is thinking as to what she is saying and doing:

> There's a two-hour stopover in Barbados, or so they tell her. Rennie finds the women's washroom in the new Muzak-slick airport and changes from her heavy clothes to a cotton dress. She examines her face in the mirror, checking for signs. In fact she looks quite well, she looks normal. (15)

What is not clear at this point and what is never entirely clear—in this novel as well as many others—is the distinction between what Rennie is presumed to be telling the narrator and what the narrator interprets or "knows" by the narrative convention of omniscience. What portion of the description of Rennie's thoughts is her own account of what she is thinking, and what does the narrator know from being able to see inside Rennie's mind, thoughts that Rennie herself may not know? To put it a different way, whose voice is speaking? And, perhaps more important, does it matter that a reader is able to identify that voice?

Rennie is a freelance journalist who travels to the Caribbean island of St. Antoine to recuperate from the physical and emotional trauma of cancer surgery. The narrative jumps back and forth in time, from her activities and relationships on St. Antoine to her life in Toronto and her childhood in Griswold. If Rennie is literally participating in a dialogue with the narrator, the reader is never privy to the narrator's response, with the result that Rennie often appears to be narrating her story to herself. But upon occasion the narrator injects herself into the text—

mostly by cues (such as "Rennie says") that remind the reader that the narrative is a story being told to her or, although less conceivably, that suggest the possibility that Rennie is telling her story to a third person and that the narrator is merely reporting on this telling. The narrative source is thus potentially plural and multilayered, and, more often than not, ambiguous. Furthermore, the narrator's discourse and Rennie's seem to be intertwined to such an extent that in the last few pages of the novel, where Rennie is imprisoned after a violent military coup, it becomes difficult to know who is speaking and, further, to know what is to be understood as truth and what as illusion. When finally the narrator begins a short passage by saying, "This is what will happen" (293), a reader cannot be certain whether this projection is Rennie's fantasy or the narrator's reporting of future events. The sudden shift to future tense adds to the mystification.

This example is not atypical of narratives in literary fiction. The problem of distinguishing and classifying different perspectives or narrative points of view is the primary objective of many prominent narratologists who seek to define the role that the narrator plays in a text, and to determine and, so far as possible, codify that narrator's relationship to the author, the characters, and the reader(s). A metaphor that figures frequently in these discussions is "voice," which functions largely to help characterize the "who" of a text: who is speaking, who is the author, who is the "I" of a text. To highlight some of the key issues involved, the next few sections contrast two distinctly different ways of approaching texts. In one paradigm, voice is a pivotal metaphor, and in the other, the use of voice is, at best, problematic. The first examples come from traditional narratology and stylistics.

Traditional Narratology

The business of traditional narratology is, in one form or another, to identify voices. In *Narrative Discourse*, Gerard Genette (1987) analyzes what he calls the "generating instance of narrative discourse" (213) or the "narrating instance" (219). To this end, he makes certain distinctions, loosely based on how verbs have been categorized (tense, mood, voice, etc.). The *mood* of a narrative, for Genette, relates to its point of view, or how the narrative perspective is organized. Genette bases his definition of narrative voice on grammatical *voice*, which is the "[m]ode of action of the verb in its relations with the subject" (cited according to Genette under *Voix* in the *Petit Robert*). Using this definition, Genette contends that the narrative subject or voice comes from "the person who carries out or submits to the actions, but [is] also the person (the same one or another) who reports it, and if need be, all those people who participate, even though passively, in this narrating activity" (213). One of Genette's primary goals is to identify and in some way define, the subjectivity that controls the narrating situation. With Atwood's *Bodily Harm,* he might seek to tease apart instances where Rennie seems to govern the narrating situation and where the anonymous narrator steps in. He might investigate both how this control is achieved and why this control is important to the story's meaning.

Genette develops a classification system that attempts to distinguish between various degrees of narrative distance, which he readily admits is problematic. The various narrative levels frequently intersect, confusing the issue and, hence, calling into question the whole enterprise of identifying and classifying. In *Bodily Harm,* the narrator sometimes blends with the character of Rennie, wherein both subjectivities intrude upon each other, resulting in a hybridization of the narrating presence. As a result it is difficult to tell who is actually speaking or to locate a speaking presence in a particular person or a particular persona.

This hybridization seems to occur more often in narratives than it might at first seem. It is a narrative conceit that a particular narrator such as Ishmael in *Moby Dick* has inside knowledge of the workings of the minds of the characters he depicts, a fairly miraculous feat since he is a character himself. It also seems quite permissible to have the subjectivity-that-narrates take on different personae as the story progresses and have (perhaps unrealistic) insight about the other characters as such an insight might suit the overarching goals of the author.

Although Genette readily includes the role of readers in the identification of these narrative levels—admitting the possibility of multiple interpretations—and although the narrative levels that Genette defines are not always discrete, one of the assumptions he seems to make is that these "narrative instances" are relatively stable forms, making their classification and description both possible and worthwhile. And while Genette is concerned primarily with literary narratives (through his frequent use of literacy examples, particularly Proust), one could easily presume that his analysis applies to all forms of narrative discourse. But consideration of other narrative genres complicates the problem of determining the narrating instance. For example, oral narratives have a teller who may or may not be the author; that teller takes over the role of the narrator, potentially fusing himself into the "narrating instance." He is physically present at the scene of the telling (although there are obvious exceptions such as audio recordings and radio transmissions); he tells the story from beginning to end; he lends a personal and literal presence to the narrating instance. In contrast to the narrator of a novel, the oral storyteller, through vocal fluctuation, attitude, or other manner, can manipulate the narrating instance in a variety of different ways, assuming a role (or roles) to serve that telling.

The character and rhetorical performance of the teller—varying as it must from presentation to presentation—necessarily constitute, if you will, another narrative level and thus a further complication in determining the narrator's function in his story. Furthermore, this level is inherently unstable, differing from teller to teller and performance to performance.

Because literary narrative, at least that which is read silently to oneself, is "authorless" in the sense that both creator and teller—as actual persons—are absent from the scene in which it is read, the problem of determining the "who" of a text is difficult. Wayne Booth tackles the problem a little differently than Genette. In *The Rhetoric of Fiction* (1961), he takes some pains to distinguish the "I" of the text (or narrator) from the implied image of the author. Perhaps the most important concept for our purposes arises from his discussion of the implied author.

> As [an author] writes, he creates not simply an ideal, impersonal "man in general" but an implied version of "himself" that is different from the implied authors we meet in other men's works. To some novelists it has seemed, indeed, that they were discovering or creating themselves as they wrote. . . . Whether we call this implied author an "official scribe," or adopt the term recently revived by Kathleen Tillotson—the author's "second self"—it is clear that the picture the reader gets of this presence is one of the author's most important effects. (71)

But while Booth makes a case in this passage for the reader's role in the determination of who or what this scribe is—and this forms the principal argument in favor of the rhetorical nature of literary discourse—his discussion in *The Rhetoric of Fiction* is still focused on what appear to be stable narrative strands or forms located in the text. Using these forms, the author creates a presence that is situated in the text, ready for the reader to uncover. Although Booth argues that this "second self" is created via the text in the mind of the reader, his focus remains largely text- and author-based. This "second self" is something an author creates as she writes (though this presence may or may not obfuscate the "real" author); it is the author's "second self," locatable (by the reader) in the text. By implication, the attention to author and text reduces the attention to the reader—a much messier concept because all readers read with different goals and in different contexts—and is potentially exacerbated by Booth's use of the voice metaphor, which he uses in reference to the implied author (or "second self").

Both Genette and Booth assume that there is some importance in making these distinctions, in unravelling these strands, in separating out the voices: who is author, who is narrator, who is implied author.

Part of the insistence may stem from the value—particular to Western culture—of being able to identify the voice that one hears and to locate presence in that voice. Perhaps these distinctions are in response to a need to replace the voice in oral storytelling with a comparable voice, to identify that voice heard in a reader's imagination—if that is indeed what occurs—when a reader reads the story. In oral storytelling, the voice we hear is the actual voice of the teller. This voice may belong to a person who is, as Plato might have it, possessed or out of his senses,[1] but it is very strongly the voice of the storyteller; it is his interpretation of the written cues. In a subsequent chapter, I maintain that if there is a *voice* at all this voice may not be locatable in a text; in fact, it may not be the voice of the author or narrator but rather the voice—often literal—of the reader in the act of reading. Interestingly, Genette alludes to this possibility in the following passage (citing Proust):

> [I]n order to read with understanding many readers require to read in their own particular fashion, and the author must not be indignant at this; on the contrary, he must leave the reader all possible liberty, because the work is ultimately, according to Proust himself, only an optical instrument the author offers the reader to help him read within himself. "For it is only out of a habit, a habit contracted from the insincere language of prefaces and dedications, that the writer speaks of 'my reader.' In reality every reader is, while he is reading, the reader of his own self." (261)

Although to my mind this would suggest shifting the emphasis of the discussion to the reader, Genette seems reluctant to do so. Proust, more than Genette, appears to be convinced of the importance not only of reading in one's own "particular fashion," but also of the relationship of that reader to the reader's own self and, by extension, to his—the reader's—world.

Seymour Chatman's *Coming to Terms* begins where Booth and Genette leave off, and, of the three, Chatman seems to acknowledge most fully the impact of the reader on narratological forms. The discussion relevant to my purposes here is Chatman's treatment of the implied author. Both Booth and Chatman see the implied author as the central organizing force in a narrative. The implied author selects what we read, and as Booth argues, "we infer him as an ideal, literary, created version of the real man; he is the sum of his own choices" (74–75). Because Booth views the implied author as a literary version of a "man," it becomes relatively unproblematic to regard what "he" says as the emanations of his "voice." Thus voice becomes an integral and highly functional part of the metaphorical scheme of an implied author. But where Booth believes that the implied author has a particular voice in the text, Chatman argues that the implied author of a text has no voice; the implied author is neither author nor narrator, but is a presence created by "reading between the lines" and hence is in part a creation of the reader. In place of implied author, Chatman would like to substitute the terms "text implication," "text instance," or "text design" (86), implying that the text provides a pattern or blueprint that serves to shape the presence that the reader images in the act of reading. Note the use of visual rather than aural metaphors; this will become important for my discussions later. Chatman claims that

> [t]he narrator, and she or he alone, is the only subject, the only "voice" of narrative discourse. The inventor of that speech, as of the speech of the characters, is the implied author. That inventor is no person, no substance, no object: it is, rather, the patterns in the text which the reader negotiates. (87)

Readers construct different inventors or implied authors for texts that have only loose connections to the real author. There is the implied author of *Bodily Harm* and there is Margaret Atwood, and these may or may not intersect as readers try to establish what the writer intended[2] and figure out for themselves what the text means.

If the inventor or implied author does not speak, or has no voice in a text, what are the implications? One of these, as Chatman argues, is that we can have a definition of a narrator that allows for nonhuman as well as human agents. We tend to anthropomorphize points of view ("point of view" being a visual metaphor, also borrowed from narratology as well as from Renaissance treatises on perspective) in other narrative modes as well as the literary. Chatman refers to the cinema, where the camera is often referred to as the "eye" and serves to anchor the point of view in the telling of a tale. "Voice" is in a similar position in that as we use it, we anthropomorphize a textual phenomenon that may or may not be centered in an individual person.[3] But it is quite likely that when we "image" the implied author or narrating instance, especially in the reading of texts, we are doing so on multiple sensory levels: we see, hear, even feel the textual interest-focus or slant or filter (Chatman's terms).[4] Thus both the eye and the voice tend to exclude other ways that we experience texts and textual personae.

But even with Chatman's inclusion of the reader in the delineation of narrative voices, he still—like other theorists—is attempting to make discrete and distinct that which might not be so, primarily because the reader—whose mercurial reading is prone to any number of influences—puts narrative identity into flux.

To illustrate the difference between these types of narrative analyses and the kind of analysis that goes beyond locating a voice or voices, consider Chatman's analysis of a short passage from Woolf's *Jacob's Room*. The passage follows.

> "So of course," wrote Betty Flanders, pressing her heels rather deeper in the sand, "there was nothing for it but to leave."
>
> Slowly welling from the point of her gold nib, pale blue ink dissolved the full stop; for there her pen stuck; her eyes fixed, and tears slowly filled them. The entire bay quivered; the lighthouse wobbled; and she had the illusion that the mast of Mr. Connor's little yacht was bending like a wax candle in the sun. She winked quickly. Accidents were awful things. She winked again. The mast was straight; the waves were regular; the lighthouse was upright; but the blot had spread.

Chatman points to the line "Accidents were awful things" as a good example of narrative shift motivating the question: who's saying this? Chatman argues that in this passage we—as readers—experience several narrative shifts; we move from a narrative position that is "outside the discourse" (147) to psycho-narration within Betty Flanders' mind; we see the bay and lighthouse quiver as she would, then emerge from this filter to hear her words. We don't know if the narrator shares her sentiment. Chatman rejects the notion that here the distinction between story world and discourse world is blurred even though the thought that accidents are awful may be shared by both narrator and character; he seems insistent about the probability of clearly tracing narrative levels or shifts.

It is not entirely clear, however, why the boundaries that Chatman tries to delineate—even if they exist—are worth locating. What is the purpose, in terms of deepening our understanding of the text, of being able to pin down the subjectivity or speaker who says "Accidents were awful things"? What does it mean if Betty Flanders thinks it, or the narrator does, or if the reader is intended to make the distinction? And what does it assume about the activity of reading that makes these demarcations important? Many narratologists seem to assume that the activity of reading invites readers into a particular subjectivity or subjectivities (see, for example, Poulet 1980), and the ability to mark these somehow helps us understand not necessarily how we process texts but the value of a literary work. But, I would argue, defining or locating the precise source of a textual subjectivity is—as Chatman would probably admit—a difficult and perhaps impossible task, so intermingled and dynamic are the subjectivities involved (author, narrator, character, reader, etc.). However we define this authorial presence or slant (Chatman) or focalization (Genette), much is, finally, left up to the reader to infer.

While one of Chatman's stated goals is to emphasize the role of the reader in the construction of narratives, he seems understandably reluctant to reconceptualize his theory in light of the reader, for this might call into question the whole enterprise of narratology. If there can be no one consistent or relatively fixed reading of a text because of different readers and different reading contexts, then the consequence is a lack of stability, rendering moot the quest for locatability.

The central problem with the positions of all three of these theorists, then, lies in their attempt to make discrete that which might be better considered in the light of its disorder. The principal arguments I have discussed thus far seem to rest on the assumption that there is great value in regarding the elements that promote textual meaning as stable (by isolating activities and setting boundaries) rather than looking at dynamic and kinetic interactions. This fairly traditional type of narratological identification seems to be inexorably bound to a New Critical approach to literary discourse that emphasizes coherence and integrity.

Dialogic Stylistics

Prefatory to some illustrations of stylistic alternatives that contrast with narratological voice, I want to set up very briefly an analytical framework using some aspects of Bakhtin, Kenneth Burke, and social construction theory that will be quite familiar to most readers versed in composition theory. I rehearse some of these concepts because they will figure importantly both in my examples in this chapter and in my arguments in the chapters to follow.

One of the problems with traditional stylistics is that it tends not to treat language as a living utterance. Essentialist attitudes toward style, exemplified by Leo Spitzer, consider style as synonymous with self, with the writer conferring on the text his own self-conception, which shapes the presentation. Linguistic-based stylistics, in contrast, tends to regard texts as sets of features that produce verifiable and quantifiable outcomes. Certain adverbial structures, for example, presumably produce predictable effects on a reader, resulting in relatively fixed interpretations (see Stanley Fish's well-known criticism of linguistic stylistics). Finally, structuralist critics look at literary language as systems of signs that, although they may shift from society to society and ideology to ideology, have certain commonalities. All of these theories imply kinds of stability; these structures are locatable, definable, and therefore relatively static.

Borrowing from Bakhtinian conceptions of language, an alternative stylistics views language as inherently social, always onstage, and always a performance engaging speakers and listeners and contexts; the speaker performs for her listener as well as for herself; the listener performs for the speaker and for himself. Thus conceptualized, one could argue that language is necessarily embroiled in infinite variation, and a stylistics based on this precept would recognize competing meanings and engage in investigations that constantly assess the relationships between words and systems of words. In so doing, readers and critics then understand better the historicity that inheres in the relationship between speaker and listener, writer and reader.

Even though literary discourse is not literally onstage, it is intrinsically theatrical. For Kenneth Burke, to view written discourse as dramatistic means to conceive of it in terms of action; to engage in dramatistic stylistics, readers, theorists, and critics investigate the ways discourses relate to one another and motivate each other. All of this occurs in the mind of the reader/listener, based on her experience of the world and of that text. That there may not be a single voice uttering a phrase but several in conjunction (author, character, narrator, reader) allows not for misreadings, misunderstandings, and misinterpretations but for multiple readings, understandings, and interpretations. Discourse is public presentation; it produces a sequence of effects and, thus, in this sense it is theatrical, ever performing.

Using the social and theatrical aspects of language, Robert Markley (1988) argues for a "dialogic stylistics" in which one of the key Bakhtinian metaphors is the carnival.

> Carnival does not know footlights in the sense that it does not acknowledge any distinction between actors and spectators. . . . Carnival is not a spectacle seen by people; they live in it and everyone participates because its very idea embraces all people. (*Rabelais and His World,* cited in Markley 23)

This notion of carnival is even more important than theatricality because it underscores the anti-authoritarianism in this type of literary investigation. There are no stable hierarchies because the linguistic and thematic elements are mercurial and changeable, impacted and altered historically and by competing meanings. Hence, the narratologist's slant, implied author, filter, and focalization are constantly in a state of flux, and it is this flux that should be the object of a new narratology, rather than a systematizing and a locating. Bakhtin (1981) points the way with his call for a new stylistics that

> [uncovers] all the available orchestrating languages in the composition of the novel, grasping the precise degree of distancing that separates each language from its most immediate semantic instantiation in the work as a whole, and the varying angles of refraction of the intentions within it, understanding their dialogic interrelationships and—finally—if there *is* direct authorial discourse, determining the heterglot background outside the work that dialogizes it. (416)

Stylistics, then, moves from determinations of precise meaning and boundaries to examinations of the fluidity (and sometimes uncertainty) of connections.

What are the implications for "voice" and how might this, for example, affect a narratological analysis of Atwood's *Bodily Harm?* First, without rejecting the types of distinctions that narratologists have developed in looking for textual persona, we would investigate the possibility of moving beyond them. To do this, we would need to resist a definitive identification of the voice we seem to perceive, especially if we are looking for a single, unitary voice that is explicit and clear-cut, and that each reader would somehow define, if only for himself. We would stop trying to locate the "who speaks" in a specific person or presence in *Bodily Harm.* Instead, we would analyze how conceptions of Rennie are affected or changed by the way she is narrated. The narration shifts from past tense to future tense; it seems to be Rennie speaking, it seems to be someone else speaking, it seems to be both. The shifts are not necessarily confusing; rather they both illustrate and point to a pluralizing of viewpoints that are not unlike a reader's multiple visions of himself and his life—at once objective and subjective to the point that these terms become easily controverted, or even conflated. The shifts also may lead to a more complex understanding of Rennie and the messiness of both her discourse and her dilemmas.

In addition, the question would become how any conception of Rennie is affected by a reader's reading of her, bringing to bear readers' judgments and ideologies. In the following passage from *Bodily Harm,* Rennie is on a glass-bottomed tourboat motoring around off St. Antoine:

> In front of Rennie is a raised ledge bordering an oblong piece of glass almost the length of the boat. Rennie leans forward and rests her arms on it. Nothing but greyish foam is visible through the glass. She's doing this, she reminds herself, so she can write about how much fun it is. *At first you may think you could get the same effect for a lot less money by putting a little Tide in your Jacuzzi. But wait.*
> Rennie waits, but the boat stops. They're quite far out. (88)

Traditional narratology would seek to distinguish the voice of Rennie from that of the narrator as well as from that of the implied author, and/or characterize the slant of the passage. It might also seek to identify that voice or point of view that controls the story. Instead of examining the source and methodology of control, I promote a stylistics that investigates the forces that inhibit control: the competing discourses and performances, and the carnivalesque where performer and performance merge. The italicized section contrasts visually with the nonitalicized; the italics are telling the reader that "this sentence is different."

But the question should not be whose voice this is, but rather how one sentence competes with or complements that which precedes it or follows it, why it competes and how it complements. The italicized passage could be sarcastic, ironic, echoing a jingle (i.e., the discourse) of an advertisement; it could be what Rennie imagines she will write about the boating excursion in a travel article. A potentially competing ideology of commercialism is also introduced. Connections are made between Tide (a detergent) and the sea, that might invoke notions of pollution as well as cleanliness, while at the same time pairing artificiality with naturalness, man-made power with the power of nature, and power with weakness, conceivably pitting the first term against the second in a manner that might be familiar to deconstructionists. In addition, the introduction of Tide changes the way a reader might look at the sea foam splashing on the glass bottom. Tide, Jacuzzi, and Rennie are the proper nouns in a passage of common nouns, calling up not only associations but disjunctions and discordances: between brand names and the generic, between a brand of soap and the generalized sea. These terms might eventually combine with other topics such as seasickness, baths, or bubbles, all introduced or discussed in the larger context of the novel itself. Each element, association, and action transforms preexisting and subsequent elements, associations, and actions; it is theatrical, dramatic, carnivalesque.

There is also a blurring of activities in the passage; thinking, saying, writing, doing, doing nothing, and waiting are at some points discrete and at others convergent. Rennie leans forward, she reminds herself, she thinks, she writes in her head, she waits. It is not that there is a lack of clarity, though one could argue that there very well might be; rather there is a contentious, disharmonious influx of sense (in "Tide," or in phrases like "for a lot less money"). To borrow another term from Bakhtin, this language, like all language, is polyglossic or many-tongued; the words are infused with meanings from other contexts. Readers make sense of it but in ways particular to their experiences and ways of reading. That each reader would come away from having read a passage with different meanings may indeed elicit the questions—if only to clear things up—Who's onstage? Who is speaking to whom? But these questions can only be preliminary. And the response can only be: any number of persons or subjectivities. It is a multi-party conversation with all the concomitant problems of cross talk, overlapping discourse, and surface confusion. But because most readers seek to make sense, the passages (like this one from *Bodily Harm*) can become the grounds on which dramatistic motivations can be investigated, generating, for example, an appraisal of the reactive nature of the italicized portion, its effect on the rest of the passage, considerations as to why this would have an impact on the writer-reader relationship, and how this might change over time and across cultures.

The Literature of the Other

Even though essays aren't as unanimously considered to be literature as they could or probably should be, I include an investigation into the narrative of the essay in this chapter to show how a dialogic stylistics can be applied in essays as well. In addition, a discussion of essayistic prose provides an appropriate segue to student writing and the composition classroom, where, of course, voice has found its most ardent supporters. For this analysis, I turn to excerpts from four essays: two professional essays that have been anthologized in a reader-rhetoric textbook for first-year college composition courses (Axelrod and Cooper's *Reading Critically, Writing Well*) and two short student essays. I will contrast conventional ways of discussing the texts drawn from narratology with the alternative approach that I have been advocating in this chapter, and attempt to demonstrate how productive the latter might be.

First, let's look at the professional essays. What follows is the opening paragraph from "When America Lost Its Innocence—Maybe" written for *Newsweek* by David Ansen:

> The fall season gets off to an auspicious, Oscar-contending start with *Quiz Show*, Robert Redford's savvy, snappy account of the TV quiz-show scandals of the late '50s. Its arrival has already provoked a favorite American question: when did we as a nation lose our innocence? It's an absurd question, of course, that assumes a homogenous "we." (Ask a Native American that, and you'll get a very early citing.) Absurd because, since this is a nation with no historical memory, every generation has its own answer. But it's a vital question nonetheless, for no country has been so obsessed with the myth of its innocence as ours. It's the clean slate from which we are able continually to reinvent ourselves, the source of what has been best in our optimistic, idealistic culture and what has kept us childish, close-minded and brutally provincial. (223–224)

Voice proponents might argue that the voice of Ansen comes through loud and clear. The narrator, although he does not figure in the narrative (note the lack of the first-person singular pronoun), is nonetheless an opinionated, authoritative, and occasionally ironic presence, one that seems to control the narrative. Although I have not included the rest of the essay here, one could assume that the remainder of the piece has the same narrative stamp, one that readers looking for a voice might readily trace back to Ansen or at least a particular persona. And although the questions that follow the excerpt in the reading anthology do not ask students to characterize Ansen as a person who is heard through his narrative, Ansen-as-narrator is implicit in many of the suggested reading activities for the student at the end of the selection. Prompts such as "Underline any language in these passages that you think [informs as well as] asserts or supports Ansen's judgment of the film" (227) focus attention on the author's presence in the text.

"Religious Diversity and the Schools" by Stephen Bates is a more formal piece, and one that sounds, as a consequence, more academic. It is excerpted from his book *Battleground,* and we could assume that it is written for a more specialized, academic audience than is Ansen's piece.

> In countless ways, today's public schools tailor the educational experience to the individual student. Handicapped students get assignments fashioned to their abilities. Pregnant students get prenatal care, and students with infants get day care. Students who lack fluency in English spend the day in bilingual classrooms. Several states excuse conscientious objectors from dissecting animals. Some districts provide schools-within-schools for students fighting drug or alcohol addiction for the children of alcoholics, and for chronic troublemakers or gang members. (375)

Here, as elsewhere, questions at the end of the excerpt ask students to identify the strategies the author uses. In important ways, the questions and prompts at the end of these chapters may be good pedagogical tools; in fact, I have frequently used similar discussion prompts myself. They do, however, often imply a narrative presence or voice, and although teachers remind students that authors adjust that voice for differing audiences and contexts, students are often asked to locate elements in the text that reveal the author's position and to identify the ways the author has constructed his voice. In order to do this successfully, stability and locatability are often givens.

What are alternatives? Granted, successful essay writing is judged by its cohesion and control. Writing teachers have developed a number of strategies to deal with cohesion (transitions, judicious repetition of key words, organization of given and new information in a sentence), but control is a more nebulous concept, and thus it becomes more difficult to identify precise features that contribute to a sense of control. In fact, being able to recognize the features of control assumes that language that is carefully managed is the most powerful rhetorically. In fact, from what we know about language and communication—a matter I will discuss in some detail in Chapter 4—words are fairly volatile things. How might it help to tackle stylistic analysis from the opposing perspective? For instance, how does the language in these passages resist control? What are these centrifugal forces (Bakhtin's term) that operate, and what is their effect? And finally, how does this help teacher, writer, literary critic?

In the "Innocence" essay, discourses seem to compete on several different levels. First, the informal lexicon including words such as *snappy* and contractions (*'50s*, *It's*), the sporadic use of the second-person singular and plural, the syntax including one sentence fragment ("Absurd because . . ."), and the imperatives ("Ask a Native American") compete with much more formal lexical and syntactical structures within the same paragraph. For example, in the sentence "It's an absurd question, of course, that assumes a homogenous 'we,'" the style retreats briefly to third person, includes vocabulary and concepts of more complexity ("homogenous") than previously in the paragraph. The text also duels on the level of specificity and generality, with the first half of the paragraph containing several proper nouns, referring to very specific things (*Quiz Show*, Robert Redford), and with the last half containing none. The result is that each level of discourse plays with oppositions that influence the effect of the whole piece so that by the end of the paragraph, *Quiz Show* becomes more than a film; it becomes a fairly complex concept, loaded with intermittently conflicting and harmonious connotations.

The value here lies in what the text can teach about language: that effective, biting, provocative texts work through oppositions and conflicts as much as (or more than) cohesion. If there is voice in a passage—and I would argue that there is not—it is so amorphous and formless that it defies definition. Even the descriptions I offered earlier ("opinionated," "authoritative") are vague, value-laden terms, and "irony" works through language play. Without a more explicit definition, voice is a useless analytical tool.

Even a more formal text, as in my second example, operates through discordances, although they are far more discrete. In the essay on religious diversity, the discursive friction works at the level of lexical elements or examples that the author gives to illustrate his point: "handicapped students," "pregnant students," "bilingual students," and "gang members." Each element—while connected in the sense that the subjects (nouns) are all students—suggests, by its presence in the text, certain questions about definitions, contexts, and affiliations that are inherently in opposition. How is a pregnant student like or unlike a bilingual student or a gang member? Are these groups to be conflated—which may be unavoidable because they are all lumped together in the same sentence—or should the reader consider them distinct and disparate? Second, the parallelism that is set up in the middle of the paragraph ("Pregnant students get prenatal care, and students with infants get day care") is countered by the lack of parallelism at the beginning and end. Rhythms are established and then dissolved even as new ones are introduced. As in literature, this is not a bad thing; the setting up and breaking of patterns doesn't create prose that is unreadable or incoherent. Rather, it makes prose interesting, dynamic, and even forceful. Significantly, the second text runs a greater risk than the first of being criticized—both by students, teachers, and theorists—as being more "academic" and, possibly, "less interesting to read." Voice proponents might argue that it doesn't have as distinct a voice as the first text, and, as a result, they might encourage their students to model their writing after the first passage. And ironically, as I have shown, the first passage may be more oppositional, conflicting, and chaotic than the second, precluding any possibility of a coherent, cohesive voice.

More often than not, the step after reading and analyzing is writing. Students are exhorted to use these professional texts—with their rhetorical strategies, elements, and voices—as models, and to develop their own voice about a topic of their choice or one of the instructor's choosing. The following are introductory paragraphs from two student essays that resulted from these instructions. They have been selected because they parallel the styles of the professional essays; one is relatively casual, and the other is more formal. The casual essay is by Mark, a first-year college composition student, in response to an assignment asking students to write a proposal for a solution.

> Have you ever been on a really tight deadline for a class project, or just remembered you forgot to put one tiny addition to your computer project; say, a database revision or a quick little bit of code to a C++ project you thought of (the code, not the project) while brushing your teeth this morning? You're sure it won't take more than a few minutes to implement the change, but you're still worried. Why? You know there's no way you're going to get to a computer to fix the "little problem." I'm at the Loop campus three times a week and like many others, I like to relax between my classes with a quick session of web browsing, just to check up on the world of technology, news, and other cool stuff some commuters don't get to see in the morning because they're too busy trying to haul their butts out of bed in time to catch the train. It hasn't been easy for me as of late, though, because there are never any computers available, even for such "little problems" as listed above!

The formal essay is from Dana, in the same class, for an assignment to write a paper in which students are asked to take a position.

> Alternative medicine has become increasingly popular throughout the past decade. People are growing more and more interested in learning information on how to take care of themselves in the best possible way. Traditional medicine has proven to effectively combat many illnesses and conditions in laboratories. However, many traditional forms of medicine are hard to understand and often have many side effects that

make the patient feel worse. People opt for alternative medicine because it is more natural and easier to understand. Most importantly, alternative medicine utilizes the patient's mind as well as body, and makes the patients a bigger part of the healing process, which are very significant and often undermined aspects of a person's health. Alternative medicine should be integrated into the health care world because it is much more straightforward than traditional medicine, and allows the patient to feel that they play a major role in the healing process.

Readers (teachers or fellow students) who might be inclined to describe writing in terms of voices would most likely contend that both papers have a "voice," although Mark's paper arguably has the stronger voice, in part because it uses the first-person singular and is more informal in lexicon and syntax. Although his paper has some syntactical disfluencies, Mark still seems "in control" of his topic and his material, lending him a relatively authoritative stance. Dana's paper conforms to more conventional and conservative approaches to the assignment; she uses an objective narrative style, and begins with a fairly traditional introduction of a problem followed by a paragraph-ending thesis. In the early sixties, when "authentic voice" was championed, Dana's paper would have been far less successful than Mark's, primarily because we don't "see much of Dana in it," a problem that I take up in Chapter 3. For the present discussion, however, let's contrast different pedagogical approaches to the papers in terms of the stylistics I laid out in the preceding pages on narratology and dialogic stylistics.

A teacher using the conventional approach might recommend that Mark take more control over his material to exorcise some of the disfluencies. He might be asked, for example to reword the first sentence to avoid the awkward parenthetical, to replace some of the colloquialisms such as "butt" or "cool stuff," or to reinforce that the problem he takes up in his essay is a serious problem that needs to be solved instead of trivializing it in the reader's eyes by suggesting that students need more time to relax. Dana, by contrast, might be asked to inject more of herself into her piece to make it more dynamic, to introduce her problem in concrete terms rather than abstract, or to define her terms ("alternative medicine," "traditional medicine," and "natural") more specifically. In this way, she could define what *she* means by these terms and make the essay less tentative and more her own. She also needs to work on style problems (verb tenses, some syntactical awkwardness), but I want to put this aside for the moment.

"Owning" and "controlling" texts is, of course, a traditional approach, but not one that very accurately incorporates dialogic stylistics. Rather, I'd like to center my suggestions around one of the most ambiguous and value-laden terms in the English language, "interesting." Students who write "interesting papers" tend to do better than other students for a variety of reasons. First, interesting papers often have "insight." They give the reader something to think about that seems fresh, new, or different. Second, they blend specific, often unique detail with a judicious amount of generalization and abstraction. Finally, they acknowledge complexity; that is, they discuss or in some way incorporate the ideas, concepts, or discourses of others. In other words, interesting papers fully involve what is different, what is oppositional, and what is contentious. There is not one voice speaking, nor is there a voice that belongs to the author. Rather, interesting papers are carnivalesque; they are performances by many actors who do not necessarily accede or acquiesce to a central autocrat (or author).

By these definitions, Mark could be advised to take more care with what is oppositional in his paper. For example, he might simplify his opening question so that subsequent sentences are more contrastive and contentious. He might reconfigure his colloquialisms to be more playful by creating starker differentiation between them and the generalizations either in this paragraph or the paragraphs to come. He might look at how his text contains a kind of action-reaction chemistry, and shape it to exploit that volatility.

Dana's problem may be that her paper attempts to be too homogenous. Sentence length, sentence complexity, and lexical choices are quite similar; there is little if any sense of the carnival at any level. As such the paragraph stays at a safe level of generality and is, as damning as it sounds, "uninteresting." She might be encouraged to view her work as a performance of multiple speakers, actors, and entertainers, and to work with, rather than against, the friction that results as the different forces meet in her discussion.

Previous to turning in this draft, Dana visited me, her teacher for the course, in despair. She admitted to having trouble writing these kinds of essays and felt completely blocked. I responded in fairly conventional ways. We discussed Dana's goals in the paper and worked to come up with examples that would clarify Dana's position. Dana might have been better helped had I encouraged her to look at her work, her ideas, and her language more dialogically, or urged her to consider her essay in the terms of contrasts, contradictions, and a sense of play. While I didn't talk to her in terms of the voice metaphor, I also did not discuss the paper in terms of a dialogic stylistics that might have helped make her paper more "interesting." As it was, she did in her revision what most conscientious students do when confronted with generic advice such as mine. She sprinkled in a few more examples and was more explicit in her conclusion.

Dana's earlier essays—more narrative and descriptive in style—demonstrated much more confidence in language play. They also contained far fewer of the syntactical anomalies than the paper under consideration here. Most of the awkwardness in the alternative medicine essay, I think, has to do with her feeling blocked and incapable of doing the job well. She wanted to achieve the same kind of control she had in her earlier papers, but exerting that control over complex material was—especially in her case—counterproductive. If she could look at it from the opposite direction and work with the ambiguity and lack of control, she might have been better off.

Certainly, these suggestions are not without potential pitfalls. Neither students nor teachers are apt suddenly to abandon the conventional wisdom that dictates that the best writers are those who exhibit a strong sense of lexical, syntactic, and semantic control in their writing—in other words, a consistent voice. And if the notions that underlie dialogic stylistics (play, performance, carnival, discursive oppositions) are introduced, what is to prevent students from writing papers that nobody—not even the student writers themselves—can understand? But total anarchy is neither what I'm advocating nor what will result if we introduce different approaches. I firmly believe that a stronger focus in the classroom on the complex ("interesting") dialogic features of language will enrich and enhance our students' understanding of the language they use, and may in important ways be a more accurate representation of what language is and does than the writer-as-autocrat model. Most writers want their work to make sense to a reader. They want what they say to be successful, whether in informing, moving, or persuading. But the search for control—the search for a voice—often results in an overly confining and constraining approach to writing.

Chances are, I have raised more questions than I have addressed in this chapter. My purpose has been twofold. First, in discussing the issue of the difficulty in locating an implied author, I hope to have demonstrated some of the problems with any emphasis on voice in narratology: how the voice metaphor can force us into conceptualizations that are limiting and characterizations of discourse that are inaccurate. Second, I have used this chapter to question the theoretical basis of a narrative theory that emphasizes stability and coherence. The following chapters are intended to elaborate upon these themes and investigate more fully the extension of the voice metaphor from literary studies into composition theory and pedagogy.

Notes

1. See Plato's criticism of oral storytellers or "rhapsodists," in *Ion*.

2. The notion of intentionality is a complex and controversial issue. Its importance varies according to the literary theory one uses to examine texts (for example, structuralist, New Critical, reader-response). See W. K. Wimsatt, *The*

Verbal Icon: Studies in the Meaning of Poetry (Lexington, KY: UP of Kentucky, 1954), 3–18 and Terry Eagleton, *Literary Theory: An Introduction* (Minneapolis: U of Minnesota P, 1983), passim. Although I will treat intentionality in a later chapter, I assume a Gricean notion of discourse that posits that intentions are social. A speaker says X intending Y with the understanding that the listener knows that by saying X the speaker intended Y. That both listener and speaker understand Y is in large part socially determined by a common culture and discourse.

3. The film/book analogy is not quite so simple. See Chatman, Chapters 8 and 9, for further discussion.

4. According to Chatman, *interest-focus* refers to a narrative effect, much like point of view, in which a reader's interest centers around a particular character. For example, Oliver Twist provides the interest-focus for his story. *Slant* refers to the narrator's attitudes and "other mental functions appropriate to the reporting function of discourse" (143). For example, the slant can be fairly neutral, highly charged, or somewhere in between. It is "judgmental commentary." *Filter* captures "something of the mediating function of a character's consciousness—perception, cognition, emotion, reverie—as events are experienced from a space within the story world" (144). In other words, filter provides the logic behind what elements of the story are presented and what are not.

Chapter Two

The Speaking Voice
and Rhetorical *Ethos*

The system of "hearing (understanding)-oneself-speak" through the phonic substance—which presents itself as the nonexterior, non-mundane, therefore nonempirical or noncontingent signifier—has necessarily dominated the history of the world during an entire epoch, and has even produced the idea of the world, the idea of world-origin, that arises from the difference between the worldly and the non-worldly, the outside and the inside, ideality and non-ideality, universal and nonuniversal, transcendental and empirical, etc. (Derrida, *Of Grammatology*, 7–8)

A definition of voice in written narratives is, as I have shown in the last chapter, difficult to determine; who speaks, who governs a text, who is the text "about" are some of those abiding questions that help fuel the work of narratologists and other literary critics. The rise of the voice concept can be traced to the transition from an oral to a literate culture and is marked by shifts in the public understanding of presence, authorship, authenticity, and rhetorical authority. Although this chapter will not attempt to recount a thorough history and evolution of these issues, I will, in citing representative examples from the development of literacy and rhetorical history, show how the notion of presence (and voice) is rooted in the prevailing status of the written word.

As was true for Chapter 1, one of my goals in this chapter is to set the scene for chapters that follow. In this case, understanding and reflecting upon selected events in the history of literacy help account for the meteoric rise of the metaphor in composition studies (Chapter 3) and its persistent influence in social perspectives of language (Chapter 4) as well as set the scene for metaphoric alternatives drawn from feminist discussions and technology (Chapters 6 and 7). While parts of this chapter may seem either sketchy or self-evident or both, they are included for the purpose of providing a blueprint for coming to terms with what voice is and what it isn't. I will look at Plato, Isocrates, and Quintilian in the Classical period, *ars dictaminis* in the medieval period, some consequences of print literacy in the seventeenth and eighteenth centuries, and Derrida in the contemporary period. Then I will point to some of the trends that move us past deconstruction, which will be explored in subsequent chapters.

Early Writing and Classical Rhetoric

Most historians who have investigated the uses of early writing agree that it was not intended to mirror spoken language. Theorists argue about its uses, but early writing seems to have been used primarily as an aid to memory,[1] serving in capacities such as record keeping, chronicling events, and identifying owners of property. But it was a skill known only to an elite few (the scribes), who were specifically trained for this function. Because of their talent for composing and deciphering religious, economic, and political inscriptions, scribes acquired a unique and revered status and were accorded considerable power within their communities. Their skill provided access to special knowledge, unavailable to outsiders or the "unlettered." That knowledge was locked up in signs (writing) and, because the process of decoding acquired a kind of mystique, the connection between a sign or symbol and ordinary language—and hence, the human voice—was remote, mysterious, and magical.

The development of the alphabet, wherein each sign or symbol represents a phoneme, promised to reduce the gap between symbol and language or between symbol and voice.[2] Alphabetic writing would eventually weaken the power of the scribes because, as a writing system, it was much easier to learn than the complex systems (hieroglyphs, ideograms, syllabaries) that predated it. The alphabet had fewer signs to learn (thirty or so in the early alphabets) and was potentially available to everyone in a given society.

By the time of Plato, writing had become more than a useful documentation practice and an aid to memory: it had become a cultural and intellectual issue. Literacy and the use of texts had important consequences for rhetoric, politics, and philosophy, some of the implications of which Plato especially recognized. At issue was the ancillary role of writing as writing developed into a system that could "stand in" for the human voice. In particular, the fact that the actual speaker could be absent from the speech scene would cause Plato to evaluate the role of writing in a civilized world.

Before I examine more fully the intersection of writing and speaking in Greek culture and the issues that Plato raises, which will eventually bring problems of authorship into play, I want to emphasize the nature of authorship in Greek rhetorical theory, primarily as it manifests itself in the rhetorical concept of *ethos*. Much of what we understand about voice today is rooted in Classical definitions and debates about the pragmatic and ethical dimensions of rhetorical *ethos;* thus it is worth examining in some detail.

In a culture that is enmeshed in what Walter Ong (1982) calls primary orality, that is, with no link to a literate world, the spoken word can conceivably have both a literal and figurative voice. First, the speaker has an actual voice with inherent vocal qualities and characteristics that are not necessarily linked to what the speaker is saying; and, second, the speaker has, or creates, a figurative voice—profoundly connected to the literal voice—or, in other words, a persona or *ethos,* that is directly tied to the rhetorical task at hand.[3] The distinctions between the two are not, however, uncontroversial. The sense of *ethos* that is conveyed to an audience in a speech cannot be entirely separated from the actual speaking voice, nor can one undervalue the impact of the actual and literal presence of the author at the site of the utterance. A "forceful" orator, for example, especially in the sense we get from Aristotle's *Rhetoric,* not only has a suitable speaking voice, but the wherewithal to manage that voice and what he says to convey a commanding and, hence, persuasive presence.

The sophistic contribution to Western concepts of rhetoric and the art of persuasion is at the crux of the issue of personal presence and rhetorical power or *ethos*. Greek rhetorical theory, especially the Aristotelian art of rhetoric, grew out of this sophistic tradition that privileges the ability to argue for any position on any given topic, transcending the vagaries of personality. The goal of sophistic rhetoric is not a revelation of a personal or foundational truth, because—and the sophistic view is well known to historians of rhetoric—the truth on any topic that involves human affairs is unknowable. Thus the emphasis of rhetorical invention shifts to discovering the available means of persuasion. The ability to fashion a particular *ethos*—one appropriate to the task of persuading—becomes an important skill and has very little to do with one's own preferences, proclivities, personality, and most important, authentic beliefs, if these are even possible to ascertain (an argument I develop in a later chapter). In fact, the whole notion of sincerity and authenticity is, as Lionel Trilling has pointed out, a relatively modern concern, first appearing in the sixteenth century, and was not a significant factor in Classical rhetorical theory.[4] But what is significant to my discussion of voice is that the individual and idiosyncratic aspects of a person or personality are not desirable and in fact could potentially interfere in the successful argument; in an important sense, *ethos* is an artificial creation, fashioned by the speaker for the occasion. A skillful rhetor needs to be able to use his rhetorical and personal strengths to "construct" his audience, that is, to make them over the way he wants, to mold their understanding into a particular point of view.

Plato's maneuvering around the value of writing is worth reviewing here. The Platonic critique of writing, as ironic or as controversial as it seems coming from a thinker for whom writing is such a central intellectual activity, provides an opportunity to examine the notion of presence in a world where writing is just beginning to take an important hold. Ostensibly, Plato distrusts writing because people who use it don't use their minds anymore; they rely instead on external marks to give them the sensation of knowing. Knowing is a highly individual matter, but it's quite difficult if not impossible to know truth without the help of an interlocutor; thus seeking truth through authentic dialogue is preferable.

Of course, Plato's position is more complicated than that. He doesn't want persuasive writing in his republic because it's less assailable. In a serious intellectual conversation (oral) you can understand your interlocutor's viewpoint and, through careful argumentation (even through rhetorical manipulation), you can change it. Writing can't talk back or change its mind; it just says the same thing again and again; it is thus dangerously out of the control of the interlocutor—the reader. And of course, the best kinds of interlocutors are wise, honorable, smart, just like Plato. Thus Plato, in his protestations, may well have had an eye toward ways of insuring political hegemony.[5]

Whatever the case, in according paramount importance to the speaker, Plato goes a long way toward conferring a privileged position to oral discourse. Writing can parade itself as being equivalent to speech, but this is only illusion. Writing may reflect, upon occasion, the internal thoughts of a particular person at a particular time, but it is relatively useless because of its externality. It is empty, devoid of the presence of the speaker, wherein truth resides. The implication is that speech, even if not internal, comes closest to a spiritual center.

In some ways for Plato, truth, and thus presence, is divine and mystical; it is out there in the realm of the ideal, and at the same time deeply internal, present in men's [sic] souls. Although truth is more often than not slipping out of human grasp, seeking it out should remain the ultimate goal of human deliberations. Truth does not exist in words, although it is our words, however feeble and imprecise as tools, that provide an access to that endpoint, that stable "thereness." Writing, in mimicking stability, gives men the sense that truth may be on the page, within words, and that it is mundane, of this world, and quickly accessible, which, of course, it often seems to be.

Ultimately, Plato's censure against writing was unsuccessful (perhaps in part because it was disingenuous). The use of writing increased, both in the number of texts and readers and in importance. My next point of reference is Isocrates, who provides an example of the shifting location of presence. For his time (he founded his own school in 393 B.C.), Isocrates takes a fairly unconventional look at the role of writing in his teachings of rhetoric by placing a much higher value on textuality than on public speaking. To some degree, this emphasis may be accounted for by the fact that although he was an exceptional speech writer, Isocrates was a very poor public speaker; he therefore may have relied on his writing to "speak for him." For example, when called upon to defend himself against a public accusation of being untrustworthy, Isocrates turns to his own written work and quotes himself to illustrate his own integrity, the implication being that his personal attributes are most apparent in his writing not his speaking. His trustworthiness (and therefore authenticity) are plainly demonstrated by the *ethos* that emanates from his written work.

Nonetheless, as Susan Miller (1989) points out in *Rescuing the Subject,* Isocrates' work embodies some glaring paradoxes. While struggling to reconcile oral discourse with written, he continues to acknowledge the primacy of speech and to argue that the voice and feelings are lost in writing. In his "Address to Philip," Isocrates writes:

> And yet I do not fail to realize what a great difference there is in persuasiveness between discourses which are spoken and those which are to be read, and that all men have assumed that the former are delivered on subjects which are important and urgent, while the latter are delivered on subjects which are composed for display and personal gain. (Isocrates 1:24–25)

Isocrates also worries about the sense of authenticity and sincerity he conveys to his audience and is clearly grappling with the debate over whether writing can communicate the intensity of energy and personal power available to speakers engaged in truly effective rhetoric. In other words, he is concerned that writing does not have the *presence* of speech, although he does not, out of hand, relegate writing to an entirely subsidiary role in rhetorical education.

The privileging of the speaking voice continued to figure importantly in Roman education, where young men were trained to be effective orators; oratory was the essential skill for a public person or statesman, and writing continued to be its handmaiden. In Quintilian's

Institutio oratoria, one of the cornerstones of this education was the reading and criticism of written texts. Whereas Plato favored an audience of hearers over an audience of readers, Quintilian maintains that good orators are also good readers since reading improves oratory in several ways. It increases the student's exposure to the language used by a variety of authors and facilitates the study of it, since reading a text—versus listening to a speech—affords the increased time to judge and evaluate, to ascertain the text's meaning and import, and to examine style. Studying written texts also provides the opportunity to commit them to memory, preserving them for "imitation" (Book X, 129) in speeches and public discourse.

The value of "exposure" to writing styles and the fact that writing is used to improve the speaking voice points to some assumptions about the workings of the mind. Somehow, writing helps alter the mind's orientations and representations, resulting in improved productive capabilities, one of which is the ability to produce more effective speeches. Effective speeches, for Quintilian, combine the logical precision that edited writing affords with the passion and intensity—or presence, one might say—of speech.

Quintilian also advocates a procedure that has currency in contemporary composition theory, whereby the student allows his written text to "sit" for a short period of time, so that when he returns to it, he sees it in a new light. The text assumes the air of being another's work (Quintilian Book X, 147). The notion that texts can be considered more objectively than orations because of the temporal (and objectifying) distance between the moment of production and the moment of scrutiny foreshadows later dichotomies (set up by Ong, Goody, and Watt and others) between literate cultures and oral cultures—that literate cultures are capable of objective thinking while cultures of primary orality are locked in subjectivity; oral cultures experience their world as perpetually present. This is a topic I take up later in this chapter.

Finally, it seems that for Quintilian good writing is persuasive writing and does not need to be spoken aloud to be effective. In fact, not only does writing help speaking, but speaking helps writing, which, departing from earlier Greek positions (Plato and Isocrates), could clearly be an end in itself. For example, Quintilian advocates repeating aloud what writers (especially student writers) have just written:

> [F]or besides that by this means what follows is better connected with what precedes, the ardor of thought, which has cooled by the delay of writing, recovers its strength anew, and, by going again over the ground, acquires new force. (Book X, 140)

Significantly, Quintilian believes that the "ardor of thought" can be present in the written word, but it is made possible primarily by stressing a very close interconnection between oral discourse and written discourse, and using the one as an aid to the other.

There are several conclusions to be gathered from these examples. First, while writing was emerging as an important force, it was still secondary to speech and oratory. Students continued to practice their writing on wax tablets as if this type or mode of discourse was not meant to be permanent but rather to lay groundwork for oratory. Second, this emphasis on writing forced a reconceptualization of discourse practices. Efforts to energize writing with the vigor (or ardor) of speech in order to make it "live" with the presence of the speaker seemed to underlie much of the doctrine of both Isocrates and Quintilian. By implication, if a writer could imbue his text with a strong rhetorical "voice" or *ethos*, then the text could potentially have the same rhetorical power as the spoken word.

While the events that I have been sketching out here demonstrate some of the historical developments in literacy that made the concept of voice in writing possible, two assumptions would ultimately be called into question, casting doubt as to the efficacy of the voice concept. One assumption, dating back to Platonic epistemology and the existence and location of a stable truth, is that presence is located in the human voice, or that it can be located at all. The other has to do with the creation of rhetorical *ethos* and the extent to which a "person" plays a role in the establishment of a written or spoken persona. One implication to be drawn from Isocrates and Quintilian is that presence is locatable or at least sensible in the human voice and that this quality can or should be translated into writing. But the problem remains as to whether or not a text can reveal its author and what this entails. It is noteworthy that at no point does Quintilian or Isocrates encourage students to use a personal voice in their writing. Students copied to learn; they wrote exordia on traditional topics, using styles developed or valued by the great writers and speakers of the period. Students did not write about themselves, nor did they engage in personal narratives. In this regard, they had no personal "voice" in their writing—at least as it seems to be understood today—nor was it desirable.

In one respect this explains a marked contrast between Quintilian and one of the current voice proponents, Peter Elbow—who in many ways is Quintilian's modern counterpart. Both are dedicated to teaching writers to write with power, relying at least to some extent on the intermingling of spoken and written modes in preparing to write. But where Elbow argues that one good way for students to find their own voice (and power) in their writing (see also Chapters 3 and 4) is to write quickly, resisting the impulse to edit and ignoring as much as possible their audience, Quintilian discourages students from rapid, extemporaneous writing, which encourages them to "[yield] to the ardor and impetuosity of their imagination" (Book X, 142). It is better, Quintilian argues, to write with care because it will result in improved coherence, one point following the next. Revising writing that has been written quickly without much thought is much more difficult to control. Quintilian, of course, is not interested in tapping into that personal, authentic voice; in fact, it is doubtful whether he would even subscribe to the concept. For Elbow, at least in his early (and still very influential) writings, a personal voice is the ultimate goal in powerful written expression.

This notion of personal voice in writing should be considered in light of two other instances from the history of literacy that are especially revealing in the ways they extend the preceding discussion. One, *ars dictaminis,* or the medieval art of letter writing, serves as an example of a rhetorical practice that was fairly typical of medieval literacy and representative of the transition period between classical concerns and the modern age of print literacy. The great change in the Middle Ages was the increase in acceptance of writing as a substitute for the human voice.

The second instance, the advent of print, was a major event in the development of literacy, and although I do not intend to undertake a discussion of all its ramifications, print literacy and the concomitant public attitudes toward the written word have important repercussions for the voice metaphor. In particular, I will focus some attention on copyrighting and the ownership of texts.

Ars Dictaminis

Ars dictaminis, one of the three medieval rhetorical arts, dealt with the growing dependence on letters, contractual agreements, administrative documents, and treaties. This "art of letter writing," which was eventually used and accepted by a wide cross-section of the population, both literate and nonliterate, is useful for my purposes because it demonstrates more clearly than the other arts (*ars praedicandi* and *ars grammatica*) the problem of absent interlocutors.

Most historians of rhetoric are well aware that writing in the Middle Ages was far from respected as a vehicle for the transmission of truth(s). Written contracts were often considered unreliable because the author was absent and neither could verify his message nor be held accountable for its contents. Gradually, however, the use of written documents and agreements increased—if only by necessity—and rules for proper contract writing and letter writing were devised, often based on Classical models. Practitioners of the art developed complex formats for letter writing with recommendations for greeting, salutation, an account of the problem or issue, argument, conclusion, and farewell, taking into consideration such elements as the status of writer vis-à-vis the sender. Rules governing letter writing grew to be extraordinarily formulaic, culminating in 1300 with Lawrence of Aquilegia and his *Practica sive usus dictaminis.* Lawrence devised a system whereby individuals who had no command of rhetorical practices (and in some instances no knowledge of the language) could, by merely copying words, devise an appropriate letter or binding contract. The system required only that the "writer" move from section to section in a sentence, paragraph, or letter, selecting from a list of prescribed alternatives. In so doing, the "writer" created, step-by-step, a suitable sentence and ultimately an entire composition, setting down in writing what he wanted to say in the proper format (salutation, narration, conclusion, etc.) while making choices along the way that were appropriate to the person to whom the letter was addressed, taking into consideration his own social station. There was no need for invention or arrangement; letter writing involved moving through a checklist.

Carried to its extreme—as it was—this development in letter writing ultimately led to the decline of *ars dictaminis,* and contributed to the rise of *ars notaria.* The task of following the proper formulas and rules in letter writing was entrusted increasingly to those deemed more dependable: special clerks, notaries, and other official record keepers, especially since a significant portion of the letters were legal documents. Even so, *ars dictaminis* was very influential in shaping public perceptions of writing and rhetoric.

This episode in rhetorical history, however oversimplified and abridged here, points to one of the permutations of constructing *ethos* in texts, one that—for historical and practical reasons (literacy rates in the Middle Ages were low and even declined during this period)—moves us very far from the human voice. Writing as a rule-governed form served a social function and was intended to be a manifestation of its human writer only for contractual obligations and in the preservation of social status and propriety. Texts carried authority by virtue of their adherence to correct form—and perhaps this is seen in modern times as an early incarnation of the nineteenth and early twentieth century's preoccupation with surface correctness—not through personal presence. And although written documents carried weight and had consequences, it would be inaccurate to say that a letter, "written" by a person who had very little rhetorical expertise, composed by chunking together unfamiliar words into phrases (that may have been awkward if not impossible for him to say), could convey either a persuasive and powerful *ethos* as Isocrates might have hoped it would, or the liveliness and vigor of speech as Quintilian urged in his precepts for a proper education.

Furthermore, texts, particularly religious texts, were generally not considered to be the production of just one person. Elizabeth Eisenstein

(1980) points to Saint Bonventura, who in the thirteenth century explained how a book is written:

> A man might write the works of others, adding and changing nothing, in which case he is simply called a "scribe" (*scriptor*). Another writes the work of others with additions which are not his own; and he is called a "compiler" (*compilator*). Another writes both others' work and his own, but with others' work in principal place, adding his own for purposes of explanation; and he is called a "commentator' (*commentator*). . . . Another writes both his own work and others' but with his own work in principal place adding others' for purposes of confirmation; and such a man should be called an "author" (*auctor*). (121–122)

While the description of an *auctor* might conform to our modern conception of author, it is not a solitary pursuit, not the emanation of one mind. In fact, writing is the result of a collective, not unlike today's scientific writing, business proposal writing, or filmmaking.

Print Literacy

The advent of print literacy effected a significant shift in the expression of voice in writing, particularly in conjunction with concomitant changes in social, political, scientific, and economic currents. Two developments that resulted from print literacy are important for my discussion here: the increased use of the vernacular in writing and the growth of the literate population that had expanded to include not only an intellectual elite but also the burgeoning middle class. Print helped expand the volume of written work that was produced as well as facilitated the dissemination of that work to a significantly larger population, one that was much more interested in reading texts written in the vernacular than in the formal language of scholarly or religious texts. Latin models, Classical and Neoclassical forms, although still the objects of admiration, ceased to be the sole ideals for literary works. As a consequence, the stage was set for writing and reading to become less formal, more diversified stylistically and more personal. Furthermore, more people—of different social groups—could have their "voices" heard.

Though the public and political nature of writing remained important, writing, over the next several hundred years, would increasingly become a private phenomenon. The period after the Restoration in England offers a particularly good example of some of the results of the privatization of the literacy experience. Not only could people read in the relative seclusion of their own homes, but writers could compose texts on personal topics in a language not so far removed from the language they used in daily life. With the emancipation of the press and abolition of censorship, not only did the reading and writing of novels increase, but a large number of journals appeared—the best known of which was Addison and Steele's *Tatler*, started in 1709—geared to appeal to the newly literate middle class.[6]

During the same period we have the appearance of the first English copyright law. The Statute of Anne, passed in 1710, provided to the author of a work or to the bookseller who owned the author's rights, fourteen years of protection against unauthorized printing. Initially, this was primarily a law that protected booksellers who were in fierce competition with one another for revenue from a growing readership. Gradually as capitalism gained a stronger foothold, authors themselves became increasingly aggressive and entrepreneurial, whereupon copyright laws were amended to protect the rights of the author as well, which would be a critical historical event for authorial voice.

One of the most famous of the proponents for increased protection for authors was Wordsworth, and his connection with the Romantic movement has vivid resonance with the emergence of voice in the late 1960s (see Chapter 3). Several important forces are at work with Wordsworth's campaign. The first was the Romantic belief that great art, particularly writing, was the emanation of one's own personal passion and an expression of a self. The second was the conviction that creative geniuses (Wordsworth among them), who happened to be magically and spiritually blessed by the talent to reveal beauty, should somehow be compensated, a notion that brings together capitalist ideology with intellectual property issues; the value of owning one's work is getting paid for it (and being lionized is nice, too). In his 1815 "Preface," Wordsworth reasons that it might take generations for a good writer to be acknowledged for his work; therefore if society wants "good books" to be published, then authors and their heirs should be remunerated and their rights protected.[7]

Thus, with this historical intersection of the spiritual with the pragmatic and the individual ego with a social and acquisitive (capitalist) world, we witness a shift away from the official and civic roles of writing and toward an environment in which, it was believed, the printed word could convey a truth from the heart, moving and persuading without the physical presence of its author by somehow transmitting metaphysically her presence—or, if you will, her voice. This feat, according to Wordsworth and others, should be acknowledged and rewarded.

Orality/Literacy and Derrida

Any consideration of the speaking "voice" and its translation into written "voice" is influenced by our perception of interiority and exteriority. Plato's epistemology rests on the theory of an ideal truth that is locatable in human souls, a truth that very often has been learned in some other life (*Meno* 85c–e). Much of the contemporary discussion about speech and writing picks up these themes about interiority and exteriority. Walter Ong, for example, argues at length about the nature of spoken language; the notion that it is inseparable from consciousness is the basis for his theory about cognitive differences between literate cultures and cultures of primary orality. I do not intend here to debate the merits or flaws in Ong's arguments, especially regarding his claims about the cognitive differences between oral and literate cultures. But the oppositions he so clearly defines emerge frequently in studies by language theorists and those involved in literacy studies, and influence current usage of the voice metaphor.

For Ong, cultures of primary orality are locked into interiority and are unable to engage in the kinds of thinking about their world that writing enables. Writing, by disengaging a speaker from his "lifeworld," is the only way a speaker can objectify experience, by being able to view it from the outside, by taking the perspective of an Other.

> In a primary oral culture, where the word has its existence only in sound, with no reference whatsoever to any visually perceptible text, and no awareness of even the possibility of such a text, the phenomenology of sound enters deeply into human beings' feel for existence, as processed by the spoken word.

The "visually perceptible text" enables disengagement more than engagement; it makes possible a certain kind of "study" (8–9), in which one can classify, analyze, and codify and, to some extent, commodify. For Plato, to study meant to engage in an exercise of the mind, an exchange with another: a dialectical conversation. It is not a solitary enterprise. While exteriority means a kind of distancing that Plato didn't want, both Ong and Plato base their arguments on the notion that "speech is inseparable from our consciousness" (9). Both would most likely agree that the fact that writing does not have the same proximity to consciousness enables different kinds of thinking and understanding in literate cultures. Plato is wary of this; although Ong sees himself as merely an observer, his argument is heavily skewed in favor of literacy and its advantages.

The notion that spoken language, because it consists of sounds, is more interior to consciousness—in fact inseparable from it—is based on what Jacques Derrida has called a "phonocentric" orientation, and this becomes a central concern both in the poststructuralist critique and in my criticism of voice. Hence I want to spend some time here laying out the relevant parameters.

Of particular important to my argument is Derrida's critique of phonocentrism and logocentrism. Western thought, Derrida argues, presumes a point of reference that language can refer to or express. This point of reference is the *logos*, the positive term, or what Derrida calls "presence," the place where the search for meaning ends. As Plato would have it, it is the form behind the appearance. Traditionally, language, that is, the live, speaking voice, the *phone*, was thought to be adequate to making *logos*, or ultimate, stable truth, present to the mind. Derrida (1976) explains that

> [w]ithin . . . logos, the original and essential link to the *phone* has never been broken. . . . As has been more or less implicitly determined, the essence of the *phone* would be immediately proximate to that which within "thought" as logos relates to "meaning," produces it, receives it, speaks it, "composes" it. If, for Aristotle, for example, "spoken words are the symbols of mental experience and written words are the symbols of spoken words" (*De interpretatione*, 1, 16a 3) it is because the voice, producer of *the first symbols*, has a relationship of essential and immediate proximity with the mind. (11)

In the logocentric view, however truth is defined, spoken language is capable of expressing it because of the "absolute proximity of voice and being, of voice and meaning of being, of voice and ideality of meaning" (12). Voice has ultimate interiority, synonymity with the self, wherein, for Descartes as well as Plato, truth is located (in our *cogito*); spoken language emanates from this voice, which is the closest thing to being. Hence, one could argue that voice is not just words. It is more central, more fundamental. By contrast, Derrida sees this logocentric voice as language and, like all languages or words, it is essentially exterior, while it is the "understanding-hearing" [*entendre*] of language that is synonymous with consciousness.

> It is not by chance that the thought of being . . . is manifested above all in the voice: in a language of words [mots]. The voice *is heard* (understood)—that undoubtedly is what is called conscience—closest to the self as the absolute effacement of the signifier: pure auto-affection that necessarily has the form of time and which does not borrow from outside of itself, in the world or in "reality," any accessory signifier, any substance of expression foreign to its own spontaneity. It is the unique experience of the signified producing itself spontaneously, from within the self and nevertheless, as signified concept, in the element of ideality of universality. (20)

The apparent purity of this emanation of voice is what gives it its sense of presence and its standing as what Derrida refers to as a "transcendental signified." Writing, because it is a *visual* translation of spoken language, does not have the same proximity in the logocentric orientation; it is exterior, outside, though it refers to that which emanates from the interior, hence the Derridian maxim that is inordinately familiar: Writing is signs of signs.

Derrida argues that the evanescence of the spoken word, the fact that it is always passing out of existence, partially illustrates why we accord it a sense of presence, and this becomes important to highlight because it helps explain the tenacity of voice as a metaphor. When I speak, I say words which I perceive to emanate directly from my own consciousness; these words are gone in a matter of seconds. As Derrida (1973) explains:

> The immediate presence results from the fact that the phenomenological "body" of the signifier seems to fade away at the very moment it is produced; it seems already to belong to the element of ideality. . . . This effacement of the sensible body and its exteriority is *for consciousness* the very form of the immediate presence of the signified. (77)

Because its instantiation has passed out of existence, any semblance of "appearance"—any parsing of it into words and sentences, disappears, hence the illusion, according to Derrida, that we're not dealing with signifiers, but rather with the pure or transcendental signified. Were speech not so ephemeral, we would be able to "study it" and demystify it; it would lose its semblance of spontaneity or its proximity to the inner world of the mind, ceasing to carry the same kind of presence or appearance of truth. Writing seems to exacerbate the situation by calling forth spoken language through phonic signs, giving us the further illusion that we can recapture the original meaning, or "pure thought." Unfortunately,

> [w]ith the possibility of progress that such an incarnation allows, there goes the ever growing risk of "forgetting" and loss of sense. It becomes more and more difficult to reconstitute the presence of the act buried under historical sedimentations. The moment of crisis is always the moment of signs. (81)

What he calls "the moment of signs" is the point where presence is most at risk because a sign is always dependent upon other signifiers for its meaning, and this applies to both writing and speech. Furthermore, a sign is always temporal, located in time and prone to "historical sedimentations," to the ever-shifting orientations of other signifiers that bear with them other historical significances or meanings based on other speakers and other contexts. Signifiers are always already loaded with a surfeit of meaning, so that even though we have the illusion this presence is pure and atemporal, it is not. Pure presence is not available to us, or if it is, Derrida argues, we can only grasp it in what he calls "traces," which are always vanishing as soon as they appear or become "present."

This illusion of presence, Derrida argues, comes from an entire period in history, beginning with Plato, in which we held to an ideal of truth and to an opposition between truth and appearance (77). Thinkers have wanted to get beyond appearance to know that stable truth, or at least to have the confidence that it exists somewhere, that there is an end to the endless deferral of reference. Because the idea of presence is so embedded in our contemporary Western thinking about the world, our language, and metaphors, it is very difficult to conceptualize other alternatives. "Voice," as one of those metaphors, is often intended to refer to a rhetorical *ethos* that functions in the shaping of a speaker's discourse and the audience's response to it. But implicitly "voice" also suggests synonymity to the speaker's consciousness.

Voice in Our Practices

Why is a critique of presence so important to a discussion of voice? The following four scenarios use voice in ways that should be familiar to teachers, language theorists, and literary critics.

Scenario A I have been the director of a university writing center for several years where one of the tasks of the writing staff has been to continually work to define their shifting roles in relation to student writers. In one particular discussion, an experienced tutor explains that she wants to help her students find their voices. I ask what she means by that. She replies, "I want to help them express themselves well in their writing so that they feel like they own it."

Scenario B In one of my first-year writing courses, we are discussing the progress students feel they have made in the course thus far. One of the students objects to the academic- or expository-style assignments, preferring the assignments that we worked on earlier in the term. She explains that the initial assignments, which contained more personal narrative, enabled her to write in her own voice. The argumentative essays were "boring" and "hard."

Scenario C A colleague is describing narrative voice to his entry-level literature course. He explains that it's the voice or the persona who controls the narrative. "You can hear it; you can feel it; you can recognize it. And it's not only different from all the other voices in the novel; it's also different from other narrative voices in other literary works."

Scenario D The 1990 edition of *The Heath Handbook* (Mulderig and Elsbreee) describes voice as follows:

> Your written voice—like your speaking voice—can vary in tone from ironic to passionate, from annoyed to outraged, from humorous to grim. . . . To a large extent, the voice in our writing depends on two relationships: our attitude toward our subject, and our attitude toward

our reader. . . . If we have clearly defined our attitude toward our subject, we have laid the groundwork for writing with an honest voice. (39–42)

All of these cases depend upon the presumption of presence. In the first scenario, the tutor is assuming that voice in writing will enable the "true self" of the writer to emerge. In the second, the student feels that personal narratives, which tend to be less formal and more personal than expository essays, enable her to use her own voice. Because this style is most like spoken language, it is "closer to consciousness"; it is also easier because of the less exacting rhetorical difficulty. Personal narratives tend to be drawn from knowledge about which the student is the expert and the reader is not. A student writer, for example, selects an event that is important in her life; she describes it for an audience that knows little if anything about her topic. For many expository or argumentative essays, the writer is not necessarily the expert, and the audience, if he is the teacher, is not only the professional writer but an authority on the topic. Consequently, the rhetorical difficulty is immense.

Scenario C, which has been covered in the previous chapter, assumes that presence is the identifiable stamp of a narrator, who is, if not a character in the story, at least a presence in the telling of the story. That presence is one of a person, with, in most cases, human characteristics and attributes, whether these be objectivity, enlightened self-interest, or blatant prejudice.

The final case tends to sidestep the issue of presence by conflating voice with stylistic choice. Yet, it ultimately comes down to an attitude (a narrative perspective or point of view) that is "honest." Whether the sense of honesty is constructed or real is irrelevant (and also dangerous—see Plato's criticism of the sophists); what is important is that the writing communicates that honesty. Good writing communicates the sense of a truth that comes straight from the human consciousness.

There are manifold repercussions to the assumptions buried within these scenarios, many of which I take up in later chapters: the problems associated with the identification of self and the notion of ownership; the emphasis on personal expression with the concomitant devaluation of "boring" academic writing; and the range of different uses that forces us to make adjustments in our understanding of voice. Among the obstacles to a blind acceptance of presence is the question of whether what a speaker says accurately reflects what lies in his consciousness, or, analogously, whether what a speaker says *only* communicates what he intends to communicate and nothing more.

The disparity between consciousness (as individual) and communication (as social) has preoccupied theorists from a variety of disciplines. Speech-act theorists like Austin and Searle have looked at the realm of communication beyond propositional discourse (pragmatics[8]), pointing out that what is implied in a sentence can alter and even contradict its propositional content. Sociolinguists and anthropologists have looked at affect and the framing of stance in shaping the perlocutionary effect of discourse, that is, the effect of the discourse on a hearer.[9] In Chapter 4, where I examine the nature of language from a social perspective, I flesh out what appears to be a necessary consequence of Derrida's theories on presence: a more historicized and contingent theory of language. Chapter 4 will, in a sense, "socialize" the concepts of discourse upon which the various rhetorical events I have discussed are based, with the goal of providing an alternative to conceptualizations of language and of writing in which voice appears to be a most suitable and persuasive metaphor. I will then explore the subsequent ramifications for the establishment of a rhetorical *ethos* in writing, calling into question the role that authenticity plays in that creation.

First, however, I want to draw voice more fully into my discussion, particularly its appearance and use in composition theory and pedagogy, in order to provide both a history and a context from which to explore its social permutations. Hence, Chapter 3 helps explain the importance, both to the American mythos and to American writing instruction, of the concept of a unique and singular voice, filled with presence, and how historical, political, and disciplinary events condition its popularity and use.

Notes

1. There has been a great deal of study about the origins of writing. An article in the *Los Angeles Times* announced that archaeologist Denise Schmandt-Besserat presented evidence that the use of tokens in accounting directly led to the development of writing (March 18, 1991: B7). For other, more detailed accounts, see John Oxenham, *Literacy: Writing, Reading and Social Organization* (London: Routledge & Kegan Paul, 1980), 19–57; Insup Taylor and M. Martin Taylor, *The Psychology of Reading* (San Diego: Academic, 1983), 17–120; Walter Ong, *Orality and Literacy* (London: Methuen, 1982), 78–138; Carl F. Kaestle, "The History of Literacy and the History of Readers," *Perspectives on Literacy*, eds. Eugene R. Kintgen, Barry M. Kroll, and Mike Rose (Carbondale: Southern Illinois UP, 1988), 95–126; and David Olson, "From Utterance to Text: The Bias of Language in Speech and Writing," *Perspectives on Literacy*, 175–189.

2. For a more detailed analysis of the impact of alphabetic writing, see the influential and controversial article by J. Goody and I. Watt, "The Consequences of Literacy," *Comparative Studies in Society and History* 5 (1962–1963), 304–345 and Walter Ong, *Orality and Literacy*, 85–93.

3. Roger Cherry ("Ethos Versus Persona") points out that *ethos* was a Greek concept while *persona* comes to us from the Romans. The two terms are not necessarily synonymous. *Persona*, he argues, comes from a literary tradition and

often refers to elements such as narrator, author, and character, while *ethos* (in Aristotelian terms) is one of the three means of persuasion.

4. For more on the rise of authenticity and sincerity as issues, see Lionel Trilling, *Sincerity and Authenticity* (Cambridge, MA: Harvard UP, 1973), 12–25 and passim. See also Marshall Berman, *The Politics of Authenticity: Radical Individualism and the Emergence of Modern Society* (New York: Atheneum, 1972).

5. For a more thorough discussion, see Gee's "The Legacies of Literacy."

6. There are a number of very good accounts of results of print literacy and the concomitant rise of the middle class. To list only a few: Jay Barrett Botsford, *English Society in the Eighteenth Century* (New York: Octagon Books, 1965); Alexandre Beljame, *Men of Letters and the English Public in the Eighteenth Century* (London: Kegan Paul, Trench, Trubner & Co., 1948); Mortimer Chambers et al., *The Western Experience Since 1600* (New York: Knopf, 1983); Robert Adams, *The Land and Literature of England: A Historical Account* (New York and London: W.W. Norton, 1983); Maurice Ashley, *England in the Seventeenth Century* (New York: Penguin, 1952).

7. See also William Wordsworth, *"To the Editor of the* Kendal Mercury," in *The Prose Works of William Wordsworth* ed. W. J. P. Owen and J. W. Snyser (Oxford: Clarendon Press), 310.

8. See Stephen C. Levinson, *Pragmatics* (Cambridge: Cambridge UP, 1983), for a thorough discussion of pragmatics as well as the classic texts by Austin and Searle including but not limited to J. L. Austin, *How To Do Things with Words* (Oxford: Clarendon Press, 1962) and J. R. Searle, *Speech Acts* (Cambridge: Cambridge UP, 1969).

9. For affect, see Elinor Ochs, *Culture and Language Development: Language Acquisition and Language Socialization in a Samoan Village* (Cambridge: Cambridge UP, 1988), 145–188. For stance, see Edward Finegan and Douglas Biber, "Styles of Stance in English: Lexical and Syntactic Marking of Epistemology and Attitude," *Text,* 9.1 (1989): 93–124.

Chapter Three

The Use of Voice in American Writing Instruction

Thus far, I have explored voice as a narrative device in the analysis of literary fiction and have surveyed the history of presence and its relation to speaking and writing. In fairly general terms, I have attempted to pull together some of the key assumptions about writing and language in order to understand why and how voice became such a powerful and widely accepted metaphor.

In this chapter, I want to narrow the focus and get closer to the heart of this project: voice in composition studies. Because tracing the historical path of influential metaphors can help explain a considerable amount about our value systems as well as value conflicts, this chapter will explore the rise of voice in writing instruction and trace the circumstances that contributed to its emergence and popularity in the United States in the late 1960s. In so doing, I also inevitably chronicle several dichotomies that have figured in earlier chapters and show through voice how they have become embedded in American thinking about writing instruction.

Antecedents to Voice

Tone

Despite its use in literary theory, any mention of voice either in composition textbooks or in theoretical discussions of composition before the late 1960s was generally confined to considerations of verbs (passive or active *voice*) or instruction about the literal speaking voice. The use of voice to refer to verbs, however, is more relevant to the voice movement in the 1960s than it has been given credit for. Active and passive voice are stylistically different; that is to say, they produce different effects. In active constructions, the agent is overt, appearing in the subject position, which for English is its most common location in the sentence. Passive constructions tend to bury the subject; the agent is either implied, as in agentless passives such as "War was waged," or it appears as the object of a prepositional phrase, usually after the preposition *by*, as in "Toxic waste was produced by the chemical manufacturer." Each form has different ramifications for how the audience understands agency, and consequently on the effect of the sentence. Active verbal constructions are often considered by stylisticians (see Joe Williams [1981] 1990) to be clearer, more dynamic, and more direct than passive constructions, both because the agent is more conspicuous and because active sentences are more familiar and therefore easier to process than passive sentences. Not surprisingly, clarity, dynamism, and directness are all features that have been ascribed to spoken language, and all have been exalted as features that are desirable in good writing. "Active voice," then, has strong affinities to values implicit in voice, especially to those values that would be important to voice pedagogists in the 1970s.

Instruction in speaking, that is, literal *voicing,* while less of a concern to teachers than writing, appears frequently in English or language arts textbooks well into the 1960s. Corbin and Perrin's *Guide to Modern English* (1955) is fairly typical, including a section aimed at improving a student's speech and speech making by considering volume, pitch, tempo, and tone, and providing appropriate exercises. Here tone is intended literally and, in fact, is a direct precursor to voice.

One of the reasons for the persistence of aural metaphors in American writing instruction may have to do with the educational emphasis on oratory, at least until the mid-1800s. Michael Halloran (1990) has traced the shift in composition pedagogy from a type of instruction that trained students to be good orators—in which writing served as an aid to good speech making or oral disputation—to instruction that focused attention on writing for writing's sake. In attending to writing as a visual medium, Halloran argues that as writing instruction became important in its own right, textual metaphors began to take the place of aural metaphors. He points to several visual metaphors, including the outline, the diagram, and metaphors having to do with architectural structure. Alonzo Reed and Brainerd Kellogg's 1894 textbook, for example, develops the well-known model of sentence diagramming to help students understand sentence structure. But while these new metaphors did indeed enter the lexicon, the aural metaphors remained powerfully in place.

Besides tone, what are these aural metaphors? In American composition handbooks that date from the late nineteenth century (well after the move from the oratorical curriculum to a literate one that Halloran indicates), common metaphors include vigor, tone, rhythm, harmony, melody, tempo, energy, and euphony. These metaphors fall into two categories. The first has to do with vigor and fluency, and includes metaphors that map oral rhetorical concepts onto writing, highlighting connections between spoken language and written language. Quintilian's recommendation to use spoken language to inject vigor into written reverberates in Brainerd Kellogg's *A Text-Book on Rhetoric*, published in 1892 (during the heyday of oratory in American writing instruction), in which he synthesizes some of the advantages in relating spoken language to written:

> **Publication,** then, among the Greeks and Romans was by the voice—DeQuincey says the voice of the actor, and that of the speaker on the *bema*, or platform. This must largely have determined (1) what kind of literature should be cultivated, and (2) the style in which this should be composed. In the main that was written which could be recited or spoken, and it was written so that it could be appreciated by the listener. . . . It is much for us that these models [furnished by Athens and Rome] were themselves shaped by the necessities of oral communication. They were to be addressed to the ear and not to the eye; their meaning and merit caught by the hearer as the speaker hurried on from sentence to sentence. Such discourse must have had, and did have, the great and essential qualities of style,—simplicity, clearness, directness, vigor. The writer who is accustomed to speaking, and who brings his sentences to this test, is the one likely to learn the secret of expression, the art of "putting things." (13–14)

Of course, oral "publication" by Greek and Roman orators who were trained specifically for oratory is quite different from speech making in a culture for which little formal training in speech is provided—apart from the odd chapter in an English handbook. In Western cultures that value literacy more than oratory (and orality), the emphasis in instruction seemed to turn to *naturalness* of spoken language to help provide fluency and cohesion. Alphonse Newcomer (1893) advises students to rely on what they do best to help improve their writing.

> [D]o not exaggerate to yourself the difficulty of writing. You can talk fluently enough by the hour; why should you not write as fluently? Be simple and natural, correcting errors when the committing of thought to writing discloses them, making improvement wherever reflection shows that improvement is possible. (112–113)

The implication here is that all students are fluent in the sense of being capable, persuasive speakers and that they should be able to translate that fluency into their writing. In much the same way some writers are said to have "a good ear," either through cultivation or innate talent.

The suggestion of innate skill is a persistent subtext with the second set of aural metaphors, that is, those that come from music. In *A Manual of Composition and Rhetoric* (1892), John S. Hart points out that a "Sentence should be so constructed as to have a Pleasing Effect on the ear" (140). He includes a section on "Harmony" in which student writers are invited to design word choice and arrangement to produce pleasing sounds, cadences, and accents. David J. Hill (1878) tells students to "[a]rrange the words so that the distribution of accent will impart *rhythm* to the movement of the sentences" (69). To help students with sentence variation and cadence, Hill cites Hugh Blair:

> A very vulgar ear will enable a writer to catch some one melody, and to form the run of his sentences according to this, which soon proves disgusting. But a just and correct ear is requisite for varying and diversifying the melody, and hence we so seldom meet with authors who are remarkably happy in his respect. (ctd. in Hill, 93–94)

That a "vulgar" ear can be corrected through instruction or that a "good" ear is a function of native talent is an issue that would problematize the voice metaphor when it emerged half a century later: Can *voice* be taught?

Personal Attitude and Personal Writing

The rise of personal experience in American writing instruction has, of course, been examined extensively elsewhere (see, for example, Robert Connors 1987), and it would be difficult, if not impossible, to do this rich history justice here. I would like, however, to demonstrate some of the ways in which notions of personal expression and personal attitude add another dimension to the associations between speech and writing, connections that foreshadow the "authentic voice" movement in the early 1970s.

In his 1892 textbook, Kellogg argues that style is determined by three factors: topic, authority, and the writer's identity. He asserts that

> [r]oom for the man himself is always to be found in his style. This truth has found extreme statement in the definition, "Style is the man" [attributed elsewhere to Buffon]. His temperament, tastes, attainments, culture—everything mental that distinguishes him as an individual— may be expressed in his use of imagery, his choice of words and his arrangement and articulation of them in the sentences, in the cast of his paragraphs, and in all else that goes to the making of style. (78)

In other words, good writing reveals to the reader not only a personal attitude but points to the person behind that attitude, that is, the author. Both function in creating a speaker's "tone of voice." In other words, style—especially style that makes appropriate use of euphony, rhythm, and energy of expression—should be markedly individual.

Personal writing has also been frequently seen as one way to get student writers to write more dynamically and fluidly. Less formal than expository writing, personal writing can reveal more of its author, implying that at their core, real people are essentially informal selves. Personal writing also tends to have more of those hallmarks of spoken language that have been frequently cited as being desirable in written prose (fluidity, naturalness, etc.). Newcomer, for example, advises students to write about what they know, not about "Napoleon and the pleasures of hope and the blessing of civilization" but rather about "your grandfather's barn." He adds, "The loving and truthful touches which you are sure to give to descriptions of this character will be worth more than all the artificial glamor your fancy may throw over 'cloud-capped towers and gorgeous palaces'" (11). Formal language, because it is impersonal, is therefore artificial.

Unfortunately, "suitable" topics are only possible when students have a choice. As Robert Connors points out, the use of personal writing in formal instruction has been controversial; instead of being held up as the goal or end-product in writing instruction, personal writing often functioned as an invention tool for the more "serious" and difficult demands of argumentative and expository prose. In addition, personal writing served as a means to an end in a crusade to inject "life" into otherwise stilted student attempts at the more formal modes. Ultimately teachers were not interested in the idiosyncratic prose that characterized the writer as an individual, different from others, or in the aspects of tone that allowed a writer to express emotions such as anger, disgust, or glee—elements that would become more acceptable (even encouraged) later. Rather their goals tended to be toward lively, clear prose in expository writing.

American Language and Literature: Celebration of the "Natural" Language

For good or ill, education is typically a conservative institution, and the American educational system, though established in a land of pioneers and revolutionaries, was no exception. In addition to the emphasis on expository writing, Hugh Blair's *Lectures on Rhetoric and Belles Lettres*, published in 1783, remained a popular textbook at the university level until the late 1800s, as did other studies of grammar, rhetoric, and oratory that used literary works—mainly British—as models for good writing and speaking and canons of good taste. In the meantime, however,

Webster, Emerson, Whitman, and others were applauding the freedom of Americans from the strictures of British traditions and unflaggingly celebrating the experiences and language of the common man. Because American writing instruction would be profoundly marked by the influence of these thinkers and events, I want to explore briefly some of this background, pointing to several events in language and literature occurring before 1900. Although not inclusive, these examples are intended to partially explain some of the characterizations of the American [1] temper as they impact some of the ideas and trends I have sketched out here. Of particular interest is the rhetoric of natural language and its connections to what has frequently been called a "Romantic" preoccupation with self in rhetoric and writing instruction (see Berlin 1984).

One of the concerns of those interested in language before 1900 was the development of a national persona. In his "What is an American?" ([1782] 1904), J. Hector St. John de Crevecoeur describes what he perceives to be the American character. Coming to the New World, he asserts, profoundly changed the psyche of American immigrants:

> Everything has tended to regenerate them: new laws, a new mode of living, a new social system; here they are become men: in Europe they were as so many useless plants, wanting vegetative mould and refreshing showers. (69)

Because this American "new world" lacked a royal court and the aristocracy-based class system that existed in Europe, the kind of contentiousness, prejudices, and class divisiveness that characterized the heterogeneous but unmanageable society of Europe (see Crevecoeur 70–71) was far less in evidence. Americans were left to their own devices in a country where they could own their own property, take responsibility for their own lives and welfare, and have a stake in the future. Thus, in important ways for Crevecoeur, Americans make themselves; character is not predetermined by any force other than a person's own will.

Some years earlier, Benjamin Franklin demonstrated how complex this creation of character can be, particularly the creation of textual character. In the opening pages of his *Autobiography,* ([1771] 1961) Benjamin Franklin tells the reader, ostensibly his son, that in writing this autobiography, he now has the occasion "of correcting in a second edition [the written version of his life] some faults of the first [his actual life]. So would I also wish to change some incidents of it for others more favourable" (16). Well aware that this written version is for posterity, he is very willing to "recall all the circumstances of [his life]; and, to render this remembrance more durable, to record them in writing," but will choose only those circumstances that reflect well on him and convey some insight on his life and times. Thus he seeks both to *create* a character for himself (in the imaginative sense of *create*), one that is acceptable to posterity, and to fashion a textual character. The etymology of *character* seems unusually germane here. The two etymological elements of *character,* one from the Latin for "mark" or "distinctive quality" and the other from the Greek "to scratch or engrave" find an uneasy synthesis with Franklin as he attempts to both "leave his mark" for posterity and "engrave" his personal legacy in print. Whether that character resembles the elusive and "real" character of its writer (Franklin himself) is not the point. The writing creates a character that can be falsified, as Franklin himself demonstrates. In a telling passage in which he describes disguising his handwriting and turning in an article anonymously for his brother's paper to fool his brother's colleagues and gain acceptance for his work, he demonstrates the problematic links between authorship, textual character, and truth (see Chapter 4 for repercussions with issues of intellectual property and plagiarism). In one sense, what he does in his autobiography is a kind of forgery, as he uses writing to create a character (or text) for himself, picking and choosing among events to recount, making coherent what might have been perplexing or inconvenient.

During this same period, oratory still seemed to maintain the upper hand in terms of rhetorical power. In his *Lectures on Elocution,* Thomas Sheridan ([1762] 1968) is critical of those who believe in the power of writing.

> Our greatest men have been trying to do that with the pen, which can only be performed by the tongue; to produce effect by the dead letter, which can never be produced but by the living voice, with its accompaniments. This is no longer mere assertion; it is no longer problematical. It has been demonstrated to the entire satisfaction of some of the wisest heads in these realms. (xii)

And—reminiscent of Quintilian—Sheridan, James Burgh, and John Rise, among others, worked to retain the oral quality in written texts in order to make them more natural, dynamic and commanding. Furthermore, they repudiated definitions of rhetoric centered on ornamentation and decoration and sought instead to turn rhetoric into the art of moving an audience emotionally and passionately.[2]

The privileging of oral language and the decline of rhetoric as pure logic or ornamentation has resonance with Noah Webster, writing a decade or so later, although from a slightly different approach. As a country of immigrants speaking multiple languages and often having quite different backgrounds, Americans needed, according to Webster, to forge a personal character or identity by "develop[ing] their own language." An important part of Webster's work is directed toward the promotion of an "American" language, one that typifies American values and accommodates American concerns. From his *Dissertations on the English Language* (1789): "Customs, habits, and *language*, as well as government, should be national. America should have her own distinct from all the world" (179). He is especially adamant that American English be distinct from British English, which, he argues, is corrupted by personal or fashionable idiosyncracies, prone to whims of the current (and passing) trends, and characterized by a wide discrepancy between formal British and the language people speak on the street. Webster's recommended prototype, the American "yeoman," speaks an English that is more "true" because more connected to the "naturally rational instincts of the common man" (75).

> On examining the language, and comparing the practice of speaking among the yeomanry of this country, with the stile of Shakespear and Addison, I am constrained to declare that the people of America, in particular the English descendants, speak the most *pure English* now known in the world. (288)

It is pure, according to Webster, because it arises from a society that despite its diversity has found homogeneity in the common circumstances of its populations. In other words, American English is presumably more pure because it arises out of the naturalness of American life. This purity makes it superior to British English, implying a strong relationship between a sense of linguistic purity and nationalistic fervor.

Of course, there are practical reasons that would help bolster the myth of harmonious uniformity in the American language. The United States began as a largely agrarian culture, many of its inhabitants sharing the same daily concerns, work ethic, needs, and values. Americans also held in common a respect for religious difference, at least in the early days of the nation, and this mutual respect presumably helped unite the society and strengthen social and cultural bonds. Also, given the similarity of concerns and the lack of a well-defined class structure, the dividing line between those who governed and those who were governed was supposedly blurred. As one of the consequences, the distinction between the language of the street (spoken language) and ("standardized") written language was less clear. One of Webster's goals was to support and sustain this phenomenon, keeping the language of common people, the farmer, the townspeople, and the frontiersman as close as possible to the "official" language of the new country.

The theme of the thoroughly American nature of American English, coupled with the homage given to spoken language and the common man, is perpetuated in the work of a number of important literary spokespersons for the American soul. Ralph Waldo Emerson's "Self-Reliance," published in 1883, refocuses attention on the self as the source both of a kind of transcendent truth and of ethical behavior.[3] Emerson implores readers to "believe in your own thought, to believe that what is true for you in your private heart is true for all men" (30). Both the reliance on oneself for locating this truth and the notion that this truth is what connects human beings with other natural beings are themes that carry us well into the twentieth century.

Another influential aspect of Emerson's work comes from his 1844 essay "The Poet." Here he maintains that the poet, more than other men, is able to connect with the "primal warblings" that become the "songs of nations" (242–243). Poetry, with its close connection to music—in its rhythm, cadences, meter—is able to celebrate more effectively than ordinary speech what men, in their preoccupations with daily living, might not be able to celebrate: their daily experience. "We do not," Emerson argues, "with sufficient plainness, or sufficient profoundness, address ourselves to life, nor dare we chant our own times and social circumstances" (262). Poets, of all people, should sing "the grand-tone of conventional life" (243).

Perhaps the best-known of these singers of American "times and social circumstances" is Walt Whitman. The opening lines of "Song of Myself" (1850) are well known.

> I celebrate myself,
> And what I assume you shall assume,
> For every atom belonging to me as good belongs to you. (32)

As the self-professed representative of the American psyche, Whitman explores what he perceives to be the essence of the American spirit. The result is a view of a national psyche composed of the actions, values, and language of the common man—firemen, bridegrooms, skippers, slaves, judges, farmers, artists, prisoners, and so forth. Whitman often champions those without formal education, not only in the characters he seeks to describe but by the informal language he chooses to use in those descriptions. "Song of Myself" is not a poem written in an erudite or highly allusive style. In fact, Whitman is eager to take heed of Longfellow's lament about overly flowery and Anglicized literary borrowings from Britain[4]: "[N]o more sky-larks or nightingales. . . . A painter might as well introduce an elephant or a rhinoceros into a New England landscape" (75). In his preface (1855) to *Leaves of Grass,* Whitman also echoes Webster: "The English [American] language befriends the grand American expression . . . it is brawny enough and limber and full enough. . . . It is the powerful language of resistance . . . it is the dialect of common sense" (25). Note that resistance will become a powerful theme that is embedded in the use of voice, both when it appeared and in the present day.

Not only does Whitman see and commune with the Americans he celebrates in "Song of Myself"; he also listens to voices: "I hear the sound of the human voice . . . a sound I love" (60). While in this use of voice he seems more literal than figurative, a few lines earlier he seems to be using quite loosely the concept of a metaphorical voice as a way of seeking and understanding the human experience he is so fond of: "My voice goes after what my eyes cannot reach, / With the twirl of my tongue I encompass worlds and volumes of worlds" (59).

Even so, voice is not a dominant metaphor in Whitman's work. Nor does he seem much interested in the singular and unique voice of the writer/poet. Rather his highly sensory, dramatic, and "brawny" language is also, in Whitman's own words, highly operatic: "I hear the chorus . . . it is a grand-opera . . . this indeed is music!" (61). Grand-opera links the themes of drama, music, language (common language), and passion for things and people American, but the voice is plural—the poet speaking for all Americans.

Style and Content: 1900–1950

The history of writing instruction between 1900 and 1950 has been amply chronicled elsewhere (see, for example, Berlin 1984, Kantor 1974, Kitzhaber 1953) and is generally characterized as a period of fluctuation and competing ideologies. Even though there have been fairly controversial efforts to categorize and define the pedagogical shifts in composition (for example, Berlin 1987, Faigley 1986, Fulkerson 1979), the fact remains that twentieth-century opinions about writing instruction were often reactionary and relatively unstable. The writing textbooks of the period reflect this shifting ground. Advocacy of personal writing is still a dominant motif, but its treatment ranges widely from discussions that separate style from content (often considered a characteristic of current-traditional rhetoric) to advice to students about using personal attitude in preparing to write (a precursor of the process movement and expressivism). In a passage reminiscent of a period in the history of rhetoric when rhetoric was reduced to decoration or embellishment, Moffett and Johnson (1937) place their recommendations about style in a section about sentences. While lamenting the reduction of style to sentencing and word choice, they still seem to want to connect style and tone with form. In a chapter entitled "Sentences and Style" they discuss at length what makes for stylistic differences between famous authors. Style is "an author's literary tone of voice," which they demonstrate by a comparative stylistic analysis of Bacon, Lamb, and Emerson (sentence length and pattern, diction, and idiom).

In his 1952 textbook, *An American Rhetoric*, William Watt tries to *untangle* style and tone, arguing that style is the mixture of ingredients while tone is the "flavor or seasoning." And while tone or "flavor" can vary by being gay, somber, literal, ironic, sentimental, or cynical, Watt maintains that a "distinctive prose style always has an authentic personal note" (302). According to Berlin, the separation of style or tone and content is possible when language is considered to be a stable entity that can stand apart from the world that it seeks to describe. In contrast, proponents of expressivism assume that a significant part of the fluency and power in writing comes from within a person; the primary goal of teachers and student writers is to tap into that natural power and get it onto the page. The application of craft and the perfecting of style come later in the writing process when the writer revises.

Despite the trends that seem to be moving in the direction of voice, the political climate up until the 1960s was not right for a whole-hearted leap into a focus on the student, student experiences, and student language. Even more recently, personal writing has been at the heart of a conflict within writing programs—both at the secondary and postsecondary levels—about the kinds of writing students should be learning.

The 1960s

According to Walker Gibson (1969), "voice" made its debut as a metaphor used to refer to something other than passive and active verbs at the Dartmouth Conference in 1966. Although it might seem that voice is a natural offspring of "tone of voice," tone and voice were not necessarily considered the same phenomena. In an article in *College English* in 1968, Taylor Stoehr attempts to make some distinctions. "Tone," he argues, "is the pervasive reflection, in written or spoken language, of an author's attitude toward his audience" (150). Tone, for example, can be indulgent, righteous, indignant, cajoling or wheedling, or shrill. Voice, on the other hand, "is the pervasive reflection, in written or spoken language, of an author's character, the marks by which we recognize his utterance as his." This difference crucially depends upon the contrast between attitude, a temporary phenomenon based on situation, context, or the author's goals, and character, which is more permanent and based on who the author is. This distinction is not easy to make in writing—because the writer is usually absent from the reading of her text.

On the other hand, in *A Practical Rhetoric of Expository Prose*, published the same year as the Dartmouth conference (1966), Thomas Kane and Leonard J. Peters attempt to equate tone and voice.

> Tone is clearly related to style, but it is not the same thing. It may be thought of as the "voice" we hear in the prose, the kind of person the author is or seems to be. Tone is determined in part by the writer's feelings about this subject—whether he is angry, sad, joyous, amused,

> serious or objective and unemotional—and in part by the attitude to-
> ward his readers and toward himself—whether he regards them as
> friends or as foes or as impartial observers, whether he thinks them
> equal, superior or inferior to himself. (132)

In fact, the blending of personal attitude and aural metaphors into *voice* is the logical next step. There are other important reasons why voice appears when it does in the late 1960s and why it is embraced with such enthusiasm in the 1970s. To help understand these reasons, an examination of some historical and disciplinary background is useful.

It is a fairly common assumption that Romanticism was, in part, a reaction against the perceived depersonalization that resulted from the increasingly mechanized and industrialized world of the eighteenth century. Although most historians and literary critics would admit that Romanticism is not just one thing or one movement, they would probably agree that English literature during this period—particularly poetry—included the following characteristics: intense concern with nature and natural objects, preoccupation with self-revelation of the speaker (poet), and the expression of personal feeling. Wordsworth's interest, for example, in "the spontaneous overflow of powerful feelings" has interesting reverberations in "New Romanticism"—a label applied perhaps cavalierly (see, for example, Berlin 1987, 44–46) but not entirely inappropriately to advocates of personal expression in writing instruction, particularly in the 1970s, as well as to those who concurrently introduced the concept of voice. In *Tradition and Reform in the Teaching of English: A History,* Arthur Applebee (1974) points to some of the key events that set the stage for a "romanticist" revival in education. In 1957, the American public's near-hysterical response to the Soviet launching of the Sputnik resulted in an injection of rigor into the school system, especially in the sciences, to try to make American students competitive on an international level. Initially, English was ignored in the avalanche of new funding, largely because English departments had, to this point, been unsuccessful at persuading the public that the study of literature could help against the Soviets. To counter this development and perhaps to insure its survival, the discipline of English was forced to make an intense effort—as it has had to do frequently in its relatively short history—to redefine itself. Two reports, "Basic Issues in the Teaching of English" (1959) and "An Articulated English Program: An Hypothesis to Test" (1959), both stemming from a "Basic Issues" conference series supported by the Ford Foundation in 1958, resulted in what Applebee calls the "academic" approach. English, it was argued, should be a field of study that emphasized the development of a technical, literary vocabulary—specifically that of the New Criticism—that could be applied to the study of specific works representing various genres and types of literature. The study of English should contribute to a student's knowledge of her heritage, and English educators should eliminate the focus on individual skills or adjustment. What students learned—when and in what sequence—was determined by the subject matter and its perceived level of difficulty, not by student interests or proclivities.

The countermovement in the late 1960s was, to some degree, a return to a kind of progressivism. Progressivism, a movement most frequently associated with John Dewey, gained popularity in the 1920s, fell into disfavor a short time later, and was resurrected again between World War I and World War II and intermittently thereafter. It has had a troubled political history, having been both lauded as education's salvation and deemed culpable for all lapses in twentieth-century schooling and the decline of American society.

Progressivism has parallels to Romanticism, promoting, albeit from a different angle, attention to personality and self-expression. Generally most proponents of progressivism professed an interest in the kind of development of the individual student that would help him function in his social contexts. While this goal may sound vague, it represents a contrast to the utilitarian skills approach that characterized much of composition instruction with its epistemological emphasis on the formulaic learning of a fairly static body of knowledge rather than concentrating on the student and her development. For literature instruction, progressivism contrasted with canonical literary education and the strictures of New Criticism with its emphasis on relatively autonomous texts. John Childs (1950) summarizes the version of progressivism that emerged after World War II as follows:

> Those educators who have combined the psychological principles of child growth with the moral principles of democracy and have developed the conception that the supreme aim of education should be the nurture of an individual who can take responsibility for his own continued growth have made an ethical contribution of lasting worth. (15)

Attention to the individual child's growth and development did not necessarily assume that the student was free to pursue any activity she wanted. Progressive education was governed by the assumption— drawn from a growing body of literature in psychology—that children learn and develop at different rates. If education were individualized, it would only be to make students—who were increasingly diverse in culture and background—better citizens in a democratic society that was struggling in a difficult world.

The 1960s was a particularly volatile period in the United States not only politically but pedagogically. The United States was involved in a disastrous and demoralizing war in Vietnam; problems of unrest on student campuses and in the inner cities were increasing; and the schools, especially in financially strapped sections of the cities, were arenas of instability and disillusionment. Racism and poverty, which had devastated the lives of a significant proportion of school-aged children, were not helped by the wretched conditions of the schools and ineffective teaching theories and methods. In English education, the value of inculcating students with a knowledge of a literary heritage—particularly from a canon that privileged white European male writers—seemed of little value to students who already were disenfranchised and had little, if any, access to the social goods enjoyed by financially secure mainstream suburban students.

The political and social instability of the period provided an opportunity for change and innovation on the part of teachers and administrators, a call that was taken up by the increasingly influential NCTE (National Council of Teachers of English, founded in 1911) in the United States and the NATE (National Association of Teachers of English) in Britain. The situation was exceptionally well-suited for a return of attention to the development of the individual student, helping him develop his own skills, imagination, and knowledge to deal with the changing world outside the school walls.

A British pedagogical model, introduced to American educators at the 1966 Dartmouth Conference (sponsored by NCTE, NATE, MLA, and the Carnegie Foundation) typified the new approach. Following the work of Piaget, Vygotsky, and George Kelly, British educators focused on the intellectual and emotional growth of the child, shifting the focus from the discipline of English studies to the student. Some of the key components of the British classroom were the following: improvised drama, imaginative writing, personal responses to literature, and informal discussion. The knowledge of a subject matter was not as important as eliciting the students' views of the world through "talk," primarily student talk that was informal, unstructured, and tentative.

In addition to a shift in emphasis, other important changes facilitated a focus on the individual. Class sizes were reduced and new ways of organizing the classroom and classroom activities emerged, including peer review, small-group work, and a deliberate reduction of the teacher's authority in favor of the student's. As a result, new kinds of textbooks had to be developed, textbooks that provided ideas, activities, and assignments for newly structured classrooms with different power dynamics. In the United States, two of the most popular texts of this period (both still popular today) were Ken Macrorie's *Telling Writing* (1968) and Peter Elbow's *Writing Without Teachers* (1973), which gave authority to the student writer in a language that was more informal and less didactic than that of their predecessors and included no explicit grammar instruction and no attempt to get students to write "academese." On the contrary, students were encouraged to write about what was important to them, often in their own individual style.

Voice and Voicism

Voice, which emerges at precisely this time in these and other textbooks, is the consummate trope to synthesize the trends I have laid out here and, perhaps more important, to shape in specific ways an understanding of what the writer does. First, the use of "voice" reflects the reinstitution of an oral component into the classroom in the form of talk—literal, active, and dramatic talk. Furthermore, this is personal talk, emphasizing not only what the student has to say but how the student says it in efforts to valorize and *author*-ize her words.

In 1969, Robert Zoellner assimilated spoken and written language into the voice metaphor in his well-known "Talk-Write" essay in *College English*. He discusses his "Principle of Intermodal Integration" in a passage that echoes Noah Webster's efforts to integrate speech and writing in a national language:

> A striking characteristic of many students' verbal behavior is that they 'sound' one way when talking, and quite another way when writing. If they have a consistent 'voice' at all, it is in the speech area. In contrast, their writing is simply congeries of words, entirely lacking in any distinguishing 'voice.' One of the objectives of the talk-write pedagogy is to overcome this modal distinction: on the one hand, the rapid alternation between vocal and scribal activity should lead to a reshaping and vitalizing of the scribal mode, so that the students' written 'voice' begins to take on some of the characteristics of the speaking 'voice.' (301)

In *The Practical Stylist* (1976), Sheridan Baker reinforces this "vocal-scribal reweld" in his suggestions for students. He argues that to find your voice

> simply try to write in the language of intelligent conversation, cleared of all the stumbles and weavings of talk. . . . [Your writing] should be alive with a human personality—yours—which is probably the most persuasive rhetorical force on earth. Good writing should have a voice, and the voice should be unmistakably your own. (8)

One of the chief complaints about academic discourse, especially student attempts at academic discourse—what Elbow in 1981 would refer to as voiceless prose (287–291) and Ken Macrorie would call "Engfish" (11–13)—is its lifelessness, its lack of spontaneity, dynamism, rhythm, and authenticity. The newly privileged position of speech and the introduction of drama in the classroom made efforts to tie spoken language to written language more explicit. Voice (and spoken language) has life because it is attached to a real speaker. For Macrorie this "life" seems to take on a dramatic, visceral dimension in a discussion—reminiscent of what Whitman writes in *Leaves of Grass*—about a paper in which a writer talks emotionally about an automobile accident.

In that paper, a truthtelling voice speaks, and its rhythms rush and build like the human mind travelling at high speed. Rhythm, rhythm, the best writing depends so much upon it. But as in dancing, you can't get rhythm by giving yourself directions. You must feel the music and let your body take its instructions. Classrooms aren't usually rhythmic places. (160)

Even though many of the classroom activities advocated by theorists to achieve "vocal-scribal rewelds," such as peer review and small-group work, were collaborative in nature, the emphasis was less on collaboration than on the development of the student as an individual. While collaboration and individual expression are not mutually exclusive, they can easily be in conflict. Working with others inevitably results in power struggles, some of them important to learn to deal with, others destructive to group or individual progress, development, and expression.

Small-group work, however, because it is less threatening and less intimidating, is, at the very least, more conducive to giving students their "voice" than traditional ways of organizing the classroom with the teacher lecturing to a group of thirty students. Although audience is ultimately an important component of Elbow's pedagogy, his "freewriting" (1973) is a way for the student to find her voice *before* presenting her writing to an audience, removing to some degree the risk that the audience, or the presence of the audience, might alter or change that voice, undermining its original power.

The emphasis on drama that the British model introduces is also, I would argue, what takes us significantly beyond tone and other aural metaphors and directly to the emergence of voice. First, the representation of emotion and feeling has a natural forum through drama, enabling classrooms to experience and observe overt emotions such as anger, frustration, jubilation—often considered aspects of tone—and analyze and imitate them. Second, and perhaps controversially, drama introduces into writing and literature classrooms the notion of role-playing, which is very important to Walker Gibson and some of the other early voice proponents. At the Dartmouth Conference, this aspect of drama was very much in evidence as indicated by John Dixon's (1967) report on the conference.

By assuming a role—taking on a stance, setting up a model—a child is trying out a version of himself and his possibilities without committing himself permanently, and as in story-telling or poem-making is both choosing and laying a basis for future choices of personality and values.

The taking on of dramatic roles, the dramatic encounter with new situations and with new possibilities of the self, is not something we *teach* children but something they bring to school for us to help them develop. Their play reminds us—if only we observe—that our verbally dominated college culture takes in only part of life and, carried into school, focuses and even repels children without our verbal confidence. To help pupils encounter life as it is, the complexity of relationships in a group and dynamic situation, there is nothing more direct and simple that we can offer them than drama. . . .

As drama develops, the learning becomes more complex. Pupils of fourteen to eighteen learn to change and reverse roles, to see the situation from many perspectives, and—in the work of writing scripts—to use the many voices of the "characters" to build within themselves an image of the complexity of the world as they know it. (37–38)

Later, in the 1990s, this aspect of role-playing is what would make it possible for voice to transcend the notion of "authentic voice" of the 1970s and find a place in a more socially oriented paradigm that values plurality and multivocality.

The popularity of voice in the 1960s and 1970s likely contributed to its lack of consistency in definition or usage. One of the hallmarks of enduring metaphors is their flexibility; they can be adapted to suit a range of often conflicting purposes. Before I connect the emerging concepts of voice with literary narrative, I want to briefly explore some of the divergent uses to which voice was put during this period.

As we have seen, Walker Gibson lays out one version. The notion of role-playing, discussed in his 1969 textbook *Persona*, stresses the disconnection between real author and textual author.

[I]t is as if the author, as he "puts on his act" for a reader, wore a kind of disguise, taking on, for a particular purpose, a character who speaks to the reader. This persona may or may not bear considerable resemblance to the real author, sitting there at his typewriter; in any case, the created speaker is certainly less complex than his human inventor. He is inferred entirely out of the language; everything we know about him comes from the words before us on the page. In this respect he is a made man, he is artificial. (3–4)

In emphasizing the artificiality of the textual persona, a term roughly equivalent to rhetorical *ethos*,[5] Gibson relies heavily on the rhetorical triangle. The speaker in the text is created for a rhetorical occasion; the text is not intended to convey the authentic personality of its author nor does it represent some transcendent truth. Rhetoric is inherently manipulative; it is used to change a listener/reader's mind.

The main thrust of many of the voicists of this period, however, was not on role-playing or putting on an act but, on the contrary, on authenticity. Ken Macrorie's *Telling Writing* (1968) emphasizes truth-telling.

All good writers speak in honest voices and tell the truth . . . not *the* truth . . . but some kind of truth—a connection between the

> things written about, the words used in the writing, and the author's experience in a world she knows well—whether in fact or dream or imagination. (160)

Here there is an unproblematic relationship between truth and honesty. Truth is a personal truth, the truth for the author. Honesty is the quality of being straightforward or sincere about that "truth" regardless of the context or readers.

Donald Stewart's *The Authentic Voice: A Pre-Writing Approach to Student Writing* (1972), another book for students written in an informative, informal style similar to Macrorie's, provides support for authentic voice that is even more explicit than Macrorie's.

> The development of an authentic voice is a natural consequence of self-discovery. As you begin to find out who you are and what you think and to be comfortable with the person you are, you learn to trust your own voice in your writing. (2)

As we have seen, power in writing is clearly connected to self-expression. The voice connected to "the person you are"—a person you can discover through writing—seems to be the polar opposite of Gibson's concept of rhetorical personae. Voice, for Stewart, is some kind of narratological "manner," a way of telling a story that not only distinguishes the writing of Mark Twain from the writing of Poe or Nathaniel Hawthorne, but distinguishes one writer from all others just as every person is different from all others. Good writers are "genuine" or authentic because they have been able to tap into that naturalness that is all their own.

> Your authentic voice is that authorial voice which sets you apart from every living human being despite the number of common or shared experiences you have with many others: it is not a copy of someone else's way of speaking or of perceiving the world. It is your way. Because you were born at a certain time, in a certain place, to certain parents, with a particular position in the family structure, you have a unique perception of your experience. All the factors of your environment plus your native intelligence and particular response to that environment differentiate you from every other person in the world. Now the closer you come to rendering your particular perception of your world in your words, the closer you will come to finding your authentic voice. (2–3)

It is worth noting, given the connection between tone and music that I laid out earlier in this chapter, that Stewart, in addition to being a dedicated teacher, was also a violin prodigy and was keenly interested in music all his life. When he heard a violinist on the radio, he could identify not only the particular artist but the type of instrument the artist was playing. This, as much as his ideas about authenticity, may have influenced his ideas on individual voice (Mrs. Donald Stewart [Patricia], personal correspondence).

In *Writing Without Teachers* (1973), Peter Elbow tries as well to help a student understand natural voice by linking writing to sound.

> In your natural way of producing words there is a sound, a texture, a rhythm—a voice—which is the main source of power in your writing. I don't know how it works, but this voice is the force that will make a reader listen to you, the energy that drives the meanings through his thick skull. Maybe you don't *like* your voice; maybe people have made fun of it. But it's the only voice you've got. It's your only source of power. . . . If you keep writing in it, it may change into something you like better. But if you abandon it, you'll likely never have a voice and never be heard. (6–7)

Here Elbow suggests that everyone has a "natural" way of talking or writing ("producing words"), and that this naturalness is the key to forceful, powerful writing because it is what is genuine. When a writer's voice doesn't have that force, practice *may* help to make it "better," implying that practice will improve upon the fluency. The voice itself will remain the same, because we only have one voice, and while it can change, it still belongs to the writer and always will.

One of the assumptions that seems to emerge most clearly in these discussions is that spoken language rather than writing is naturally closer to consciousness and to presence—a concept I discussed in the last chapter. The best writing taps directly into the spoken word and consequently gets closest to what's real, genuine, legitimate, and does so in the most powerful way, through personal presence.

Before I build on my discussion in Chapter 2 and examine how this perspective has been modified in composition studies in the last two decades, I want to briefly discuss a third dichotomy embedded within the voice metaphor, that of the nature of expository writing and its connection with creative writing and literary or essayist narratives. This connection, I believe, may provide a clue to understanding the scope and power of voice.

The Literary Narrative

While voice is widely used in composition, it appeared much earlier in literary and rhetorical criticism. Wayne Booth and T. S. Eliot used voice to talk about literary language. In Booth's *The Rhetoric of Fiction* (1961), voice refers to authorial narrative (reliable, unreliable, dramatized, etc.). T. S. Eliot, in "The Three Voices of Poetry" (1943) says, "In writing [nondramatic] verse, I think that one is writing, so to speak, in terms of one's own voice: the way it sounds when you read it to yourself is the test. For it is yourself speaking. The question of communication, of what the reader will get from it, is not paramount" (100).

For complex reasons that have been widely discussed elsewhere (see, for example, Scholes 1985, Phelps 1988), literary texts tend to be more highly regarded both within the academy and outside it than non-literary texts. This bias extends to student writing, where creative writing even by novice writers is frequently more highly valued than student expository prose. Embedded in Walker Gibson's pedagogy is the assumption that the strongest kinds of voices are literary voices, and he is not alone. The use of literary works as models of good writing occurs quite frequently. Although just what distinguishes "literary" writing from "nonliterary" writing is already problematic, the concept of authentic prose, or prose with a voice, seems to run parallel to a sense of its literariness. In an earlier article in 1962, Gibson argues that literary texts provide good models for how writers create a voice, and the majority of writing samples he provides in *Persona* are from novels or short stories (even poems). These voices, Gibson maintains, are dramatic, creative, and unique—all features of both the British model of education as well as the "voicist" program of Elbow, Macrorie, William E. Coles, Jr., Donald Stewart, Donald Murray, and others.

Creative, personal writing (the paradigmatic example seems to be the literary narrative) is very important to the most familiar concept of voice that appeared in the early 1970s, that of personal voice. As voicists consider and examine types of prose writing—both student writing and professional texts—that reputedly have voice, very often their examples are (or substantially contain) dramatic narratives. For how does one convey a personal attitude? One of the most obvious ways is to use the first-person singular, "I," to relate one's discussion to personal events, and to display passion or emotion. Students who tell personal stories about their lives, experiences, and important personal events in dramatic, less formal (nonacademic) ways are the students who seem to do the best in voicist pedagogies. This implicit privileging of the dramatic narrative form is evident in the classroom that William Coles describes in *The Plural I* (1978). The kinds of essays that receive the most positive attention from him are personal essays that include narratives with colorful description and dialogue, all of which convey some kind of impassioned belief about some event or experience. By contrast, the essays that receive the most scathing attacks are essays that "don't sound" like the author. For example, after his class has read a lucid and well-crafted student essay on the meaning of "amateur" and "professional," Coles reportedly asks one of the student readers, "How about it Jim, do you talk that way?" Jim, of course, says, "No," and the class consequently determines that the author of the essay sounds phoney (objective, academic). Favorably reviewed essays in Coles' class reveal "genuine" passion.

Unfortunately, emotive language and passionate display aren't very enthusiastically endorsed for expository and argumentative prose. Whether short-sighted or not, passionate language is almost by definition less rational (i.e., less reasoned) than the more "objective" academic prose and, hence, less persuasive and less desirable for the kinds of commerce that students and academic writers deal in. If emotionally charged language is more conducive to revealing a self, then one is left to assume that one's true self consists more of feeling than of objective and reasoned thinking, a presumption that, at its heart, even voicists would have trouble agreeing with.

As well as the dubious endorsement of passionate display over detached (academic) prose, there is another more troubling dimension to this emerging dichotomy. This "genuineness" seems largely determined by the class and the instructor, so that the power in shaping a text is, ironically, out of the hands of the student; the student must shape his essay to sound "genuine" or "authentic" to the audience (see Elizabeth Ellsworth's [1989] well-known critique of critical pedagogy). Hence, we revert to a paradigm where the audience creates (or co-creates) authenticity in the writer.

I don't mean to suggest here that one should discourage dramatic writing or efforts to write in impassioned ways about a topic. What I am hoping to underscore is the tacit privileging of a specific genre—the narrative—and the implied message to students that they should resist the temptation to learn to write traditional academic prose. The hallmark of personal power (at least for voicists like Elbow, Coles, Macrorie, and others) becomes the discovery and deployment of a *personal* voice in writing. By extension, the student is encouraged by these voicists *not* to join the ranks of the academic elite who write vacuous, empty prose, but to acquire power by promoting their unique selves.

With voice, we uphold the following values:

1. good writing as personal, individual, unique;
2. good writing as the intermingling of oral and written modes, with oral becoming the favored term;
3. good writing as having the dramatic qualities of narrative, especially literary narrative, the prototype for which, of course, is the earliest form of literature in oral, preliterate cultures, that is, storytelling.

This period in the 1960s and early 1970s is not the first example of the confluence of the pedagogical moves that I have outlined. The decline of oratory in eighteenth-century United States paralleled the rise of belletristic rhetoric, a shift that was also accompanied, Halloran points out, by a shift toward the personal, reflecting a growing concern for private, individual experience. But the principal concerns contrast sharply with those of the 1970s. In the eighteenth and nineteenth centuries, belletristic rhetoric focused on eloquence, and education was geared toward developing "taste," especially important in a climate of class mobility. Voice emerges when it does in the 1970s for different historical reasons; personal writing now *is* a desired end product. Personal expression emerges as the ultimate in rhetorical power, and spoken language—the human voice—is the best source of this power.

The Problem with Voice

In using voice to refer to writing, we have made a conceptual leap, one that has been relentlessly assailed by poststructuralists, as I have discussed at some length. Many voice proponents tend to equate identifiability with identity and assume that the features we recognize in the speech exchange represent the authentic emanation of the human mind, wherein exists the core of that individual, her "truth." The poststructuralist critique calls this supposition into question, making voice a kind of dinosaur.

Another related assumption underlying the authentic voice pedagogy that is equally disputable is that language is social in only limited ways, that ultimately the individual can (and in some cases should) be isolated from the social uses of language—especially in the invention and drafting stages—and that this enables the cultivation of a particular voice. The social construction movement seems to have reduced the attention on individual voices—in fact has called into question whether or not we can or even should attempt to identify a self that is separate or discrete from its social context—in favor of an emphasis on rhetorical interaction.

Most of the arguments I have drawn into this discussion have been made before, much more thoroughly and in much greater detail than I have been able to do here. But herein lies the point that underlies this project; *voice* connects us to a number of trends central to our study of language (speech and writing, individual and social perspective, literature and composition). Perhaps the most important conclusion to be drawn in an examination of the confluences of these trends has to do with a kind of conflict of interest; that is, even in the post-oratorical, post-expressionist, postmodern mood that seems to guide much of our thinking today, we are still preoccupied with voice, perpetuating a trend begun in the early days of writing. We continue to use terminology from an oral mode to refer to, make sense of, and shape our perceptions about a written mode. If the reason for this is not simply the sluggish nature of language change, and I don't think it is, then what is it? Does "voice" really offer us and our students ways of approaching language that are at least helpful if not insightful? I think it does not, and I will spend the next chapter making this case.

It is perhaps a truism to say that metaphors endure for good reasons. For example, the common metaphorical expression "Time is money" makes sense (at least in our modern capitalist society) because culturally it is easy to connect the two. Time is readily viewed in terms of money; people get paid for time they "spend" on the job—often on an incremental, hourly basis—and work is frequently valued in terms of how much money can be earned per hour. The one, then, helps us conceive of the other and guides our thinking about it. Voice operates in the same way. Voice helps writers conceptualize some of the intangibles in writing, helping make concrete such abstractions as meaning, power, liveliness, honesty. Voice continues to maintain its allure in composition pedagogy quite possibly because it appeals to other values (often implicit rather than explicit) that both educators and students already hold. These values include the importance of writers as individuals (privileged over social or rhetorical concerns), the power of the speech (privileged over writing), the force of the literary narrative (privileged over other genres such as the expository or critical essay).

But all metaphors foreclose on other ways of perceiving experience. Thus, it becomes important to question why and how we use metaphors, and to assess their merits in terms of changing goals, ideas, and values, especially those metaphors involved in something as consequential as teaching writing. If, for example, one subscribes to a social view of language, especially a Bakhtinian view that maintains that all discourse is inhabited by meaning from other contexts and uses, then the voice metaphor (which Bakhtin himself uses—problematically, I will argue in Chapter 4) ceases to function effectively. That is, if discourse is never only the product or property of one individual, then some of the values implicit in the voice metaphor do not correspond.

Alternatives, however, are not easy to discover. Style, for example, is perhaps a more neutral term. Moreover, because it comes from the Latin *stylus,* a pointed instrument with which the ancients wrote on wax tablets, style is a metaphor derived from writing, not from speech. But many writers have argued that style is not the same as tone (which, for some, is not the same as voice). Ken Macrorie quotes Mary McCarthy from the Paris Review's *Writers at Work* series:

> I've never liked the conventional conception of "style." What's confusing is that style usually means some form of fancy writing—when people say, oh yes, so and so's such a "wonderful stylist." But if one means by style the voice, the irreducible and always recognizable and alive thing, then of course style is really everything. (in Macrorie 161)

The distinctions are potentially endless and often more confusing than illuminating.

I am not necessarily advocating here that we summarily do away with metaphors that don't fit our theoretical inclinations. Despite injunctions to the contrary, mixing metaphors may not be so bad. Rather I am arguing that we question how metaphors work and what they communicate about what writing is and does. For it may be that as we mix metaphors in our composition textbooks, we are also mixing the messages we send to our students.

Notes

1. Note that in using the term "American," I am deliberately using it as the major writers of the period (Crevecoeur, Webster, Emerson) used it. *American* then refers largely to the white male population of the United States (and possibly Canada) and generally excludes Native American, African American, and Central and South American. White women are generally implicit in use of the term "men."

2. See Jay Fliegelman's *Declaring Independence: Jefferson, Natural Language, and the Culture of Performance* (Stanford, CA: Stanford University Press, 1993) and Kenneth Cmiel's *Democratic Eloquence: The Fight over Popular Speech in Nineteenth-Century America* (New York: W. Morrow, 1990) for more thorough discussions about what has been called the elocutionary revolution in America.

3. See also Berlin (1984), 42–57.

4. From his review of Sidney's *Defence of Poetry* (1832).

5. See Cherry (1994) for different ways of looking at persona.

Chapter 4

Toward a Social
Definition of Voice

The Individual Voice

One of the reasons voice is so difficult to criticize effectively is that it is intensely mercurial. It is, for example, at once synecdoche, metonymy, and metaphor. Authentic voice proponents use voice synechdochically, as a significant feature of a whole person, a physical component that helps constitute and identify who that person is. Metonymically, voice is less of a physical feature than an attribute, facilitating conceptions of voice as a rhetorical persona that is featured for occasions and situations, and thus is a phenomenon that can be changed and adjusted; it is not necessarily anchored to a personality or identity. In a larger, metaphoric sense, voice is used in place of something else to highlight or accentuate connections (as between spoken language and written language). Obviously, these tropes, like many others, are not discrete and are in fact analogs, connected by the root word (*voice*) as well as associations that have accrued through common usage. These connections both enrich voice and complicate it.

In this chapter, using the now very familiar social perspectives of Bakhtin and other language theorists, I want to call into question all these uses of voice. In so doing, I will show how even the modern uses of voice—as choral voices, dialogic voices, or as voices in response—suffer from the same kinds of dilemmas as the oft-criticized authentic voice. I begin with an example that typifies some of the complexity as it conflates the notion of authentic voice with plural voices. This provides a useful point of departure for examining what it means to create authorial identity.

When Toby Fulwiler (1990) writes of his quest to find his own voice in his writing, he defines "voice" as "some identifying tone or timbre that makes us conscious of the author's presence, that lets us *hear* the person behind the sentences" (214). First, and perhaps foremost, the notion that readers can identify authors through their discourse requires considerable scrutiny. Can a "person" be recognized on the basis of a "tone" or "timbre"? If so, what do we recognize? Is this self for Fulwiler a fixed entity, or is it a rhetorical projection, unique to a specific rhetorical situation? What does it mean to be a "person" or, on the other hand, a "writing-person" or "speaking-person," and are they the same? Foucault (1977) raises a more fundamental question in the last paragraph of "What Is an Author?" Regarding the enterprise to understand who and what an author is, he asks, "Does it matter?"

As is readily apparent by now, spoken language can reveal its speaker in a way that writing cannot. We can locate the source of the sound; the physicality of voice identifies the speaking person. A listener can identify not only who speaks but a great many other attributes of the speaker that influence the meaning of the speech exchange (the speaker's fluency, mood, emphasis, age, gender, health, sobriety, etc.). Writing is much more problematic because the author, as a physical presence, is separated from her text; she is absent from the scene of reading of a text that she has most likely had the luxury to revise.

Even as Fulwiler examines the different genres in which he writes, he recognizes that his writing persona is, at least in some respects, dependent upon a specific writing context to inform its character. The voice in his journals differs from the voice in his academic, published discourse, which is quite unlike his voice in creative writing. He admits that "[i]f there is such a thing as an authentic voice, it is protean and shifty" (218), adaptable to new situations and demands. He also acknowledges the degree to which his voice is influenced by the different communities in which he writes. Nevertheless, he insists that he can recognize in much of his writing, especially the writing he values, an identifiable writing voice, and it is distinct from the voices of other writers. He points out that writers should be encouraged to seek out and develop the voice that is "authentically" their own (216), an assumption that permeates composition theory, especially the work of Peter Elbow, and is often embraced by "creative" writers. In much the same way, literary critics often seek to identify that "voice" that is authentically Shakespeare's or Hemingway's under the supposition that the Hemingway persona is distinct from that of another writer and that there is an importance in making that distinction.

In assessing how much impact human beings have on the language they use, we should question the degree of power authors have to infuse texts with their personal and idiosyncratic selves. The assumption that language is first and foremost a social activity seems to be obscured by the use of voice, which, I believe, reinforces a generally Western emphasis on individuality and inspires the quest to advance a personal and unique self through one's rhetoric.

Foucault may have located part of the reason for the infatuation with voice. One of his tasks in *The Archaeology of Knowledge* (1972) is to attempt to reduce our preoccupation with the author or the speaking subject. The problem, he writes, is as follows:

> [People find] it difficult enough to recognize that their history, their economics, their social practices, the language (*langue*) that they speak, the mythology of their ancestors, even the stories that they were told in their childhood, are governed by rules that are not all given to their consciousness; they can hardly agree to being dispossessed in addition of that discourse in which they wish to be able to say immediately and directly what they think, believe, or imagine; they prefer to deny that discourse is a complex, differentiated practice, governed by analyzable rules and transformations, rather than be deprived of that tender, consoling certainty of being able to change, if not the world, if not life, at least their 'meaning,' simply with a fresh word that can come only from themselves, and remain for ever close to the source. (210–211)

If we relinquish the notion that we are the ultimate arbiters of our lives and language, that we are prone in large respect to the controlling influences of environments, contexts, and other people, we should also call into question a fundamental component of the Western self-conception: unfettered free will. While we are not necessarily powerless, neither are we free. It might be more helpful, in fact, if we redefined power (as in "powerful writing" or "powerful speaking") in terms that are more strongly suggestive of the ongoing dialogue in which we participate daily, instead of equating power with freedom to act and speak precisely as we like.

Before I go further, two terms, *rhetorical persona* and *individual voice*, both of which impact how selves are connected to utterances, need to be untangled. Echoing an earlier claim by Walker Gibson, an author creates a "persona" for a specific occasion, just as a speaker engages in role-playing in the determination of the type of face or front he wants to present to an audience.[1] A "person" on the other hand is a collection of traits, attitudes, and dispositions that is the force *behind* the presentational self, or persona. One's status as a person is a product of one's rhetorical power. Personhood is a status conferred by the community of which we are members—by our work, our family, our friends, our clubs and affiliations—and it is also effected by what these communities value, such as belongings, wealth, social background. Thus, a person is, in large part, a rhetorical creation, that is, the style and accumulation of roles he plays or is forced to play and how his community perceives him via these roles. Although at his core, a person may or may not be a stable entity or speak with a consistent individual voice, the point is moot, for he is identified by rhetorical positions, and these are neither fixed nor necessarily consistent. By this argument, it would be difficult to maintain that a person, through some identifying tone or timbre, can be "heard" behind his words, for his words are part of the presentational, role-playing self that is created for occasions and communities.

Individual Voices and Vygotsky

The work done in language development, especially that by Jean Piaget and Lev Vygotsky, provides some insight into the problematic relation of self and persona. Piaget tends to look at individualist perspectives of cognitive development, while Vygotsky nests both language and intellectual development into a decidedly social context. These two different positions, while not polar opposites, frame the construction of self differently, and as a consequence see the self's relationship to the outside world, which one could almost construe as a persona (or presentational self), in two quite different ways.

Piaget explored aspects of the formation of self in children, maintaining that crucial stages in development are private operations that the child undergoes alone, and are not necessarily associated with language. Language, Piaget insists, is only one form of representational intelligence and makes little or no qualitative contribution to the maturation of thinking processes. Specifically, he argues that the transition from sensorimotor (eighteen to twenty-four months) to representational intelligence in children occurs without the involvement of language. In the latter stages of sensorimotor development, children typically begin to use language; they learn that words refer to objects, that words are symbols. At this stage the child develops egocentric speech, the character of which is determined by the fact that she is not yet capable of taking the point of view of the other. Piaget felt that egocentric speech was the verbalization of the child's thought rather than any attempt to engage or respond to others (other children or caregivers), assuming that important aspects of the human psyche are formed without social mediation or the input of "an other."

In *Thought and Language*, Vygotsky suggests that Piaget may not have given sufficient consideration to the influence of language on the cognitive development of the child. Vygotsky argues that language and thought may have their own identities, yet once they converge in the development of a child, there is a qualitative change not merely in a child's cognition, but in her language as well; egocentric speech has an important social component. His experiments with children (who were

at Piaget's sensorimotor stage), suggested that the presence of others—
in other words, having an audience—has a dramatic impact on what
was occurring. When a child has no audience, the child stops verbaliz-
ing. Vygotsky concluded that even in its earliest stages, a child's speech
is social; she communicates with persons around her such as parents,
siblings, playmates. Gradually, that social speech becomes internalized
into what Vygotsky calls "inner speech." He argued that Piaget's "egocentric speech" was really a stage of development where social speech
was becoming internalized, where the child was beginning to use language in thought. At this stage, the child begins to use language for himself to self-regulate, taking over the linguistic role of monitor that the
adult previously held. The process continues until inner speech becomes
quite different from external speech.

The shift from the early stages of outer, social speech to inner
speech has ramifications, particularly for champions of authentic voice.
Vygotsky writes:

> If we compare the early development of speech and intellect with the
> development of inner speech and verbal thought, we must conclude
> that the later stage is not a simple continuation of the earlier. *The na-
> ture of the development itself changes,* from biological to sociohistorical.
> Verbal thought is not an innate, natural form of behavior, but is de-
> termined by a historical-cultural process and has specific properties
> and laws that cannot be found in the natural forms of thought and
> speech. (1986, 94)

Cognitive development, then, occurs on two planes, first the social
plane (with others), and then the psychological (within the child). So
while much of development occurs within the mind of the child, it has
from very early on been socially mediated, and whatever is "authentic"
or "genuine" or even original about a person, even at this early stage,
has been largely influenced by the language of others—including motivations and intentions—and ceases to have the kind of purity that we
have come to associate with authenticity.

Ultimately, inner speech becomes quite different from the speech
produced for others. Many of the characteristics of inner speech imply
a strong dialectical dynamic not only between a speaker and a potential audience but between speaker and environment. For example, inner speech is regularly abbreviated, disconnected, and incomplete; a
great deal of information is omitted because it is supplied by the social context. Likewise the constructions are predicate-heavy; that is, the
subject of a sentence and all the words connected to it are omitted. These
phenomena occur regularly in speech acts where the context, previously acquired knowledge, and other speakers and their mutual knowledge and shared history provide the missing information. In a person's

inner speech, the *sense* of a word—often supplied and connected to psychological events—is more important than its referential meaning. The sense of a word is influenced as well by other language in the context. Hence, words become more highly charged emotionally and psychologically than they might be if the child was merely incorporating referential meanings into his personal lexicon. In inner speech, the speaker is reshaping language as much as language is reshaping her; the enterprise is highly cooperative.

If we accept Vygotsky's argument, then one of the central dichotomies implied earlier, that of internal as "mine" and external as "social," is called into question, at least in cognitive development. The notion of the internal as thought and the external as language—shaped by the internal—can no longer be viewed as discrete; rather as the distinctions become less clear, a different way of thinking about language and thought emerges, one where interaction and the capacity for mutual transformation are significant features.

Vygotsky's argument also provides a basis for the claim I made earlier that the "person" (speaker or writer) is socially mediated on a fundamental level. As such, the speaking/writing person is "protean" and "shifty" because the nature of human existence is such, changing as contexts, speakers, and listeners change. That speakers have the ability to use different language variations in different contexts, or that they have the ability to choose to keep their own counsel, or to hold internal conversations as they weigh difficult decisions or sort out problems all, ultimately, grow out of this interaction between the individual and the social. Neither language nor thought can be purely the result of an ego in isolation, even when a speaker appears to be in charge of his own consciousness and thought.

Bakhtin and Dialogic Voices

Much of the work done by Vygotsky in language acquisition and cognitive development reverberates in the perspectives of M. M. Bakhtin, and an examination of some of Bakhtin's arguments may provide further insight on the problem of social and personal discourses. Because Bakhtin's theory of language is well known, I will merely summarize his main tenets to lay some groundwork. His central argument in *The Dialogic Imagination* is that discourse operates dialogically, and that while this is most supremely apparent in the novel, it is also a feature of all discourse (with the possible exception of poetry). The substance of his argument that is relevant to voice is this: Each word or phrase we use interacts with, changes, and is changed by the other words, phrases, and discourses that it encounters, whether in speech or in writing. Words alter and are altered by surrounding words in a sentence as well as shifting in meaning over time and context, or historically (cf. Derrida's "historical sedimentation" in Chapter 2). Not only does a writer, for example, transform the meaning of every other word in a sentence when he adds a word to the sentence, but because that sentence is changed, so is the meaning of his paragraph and, hence, his entire text. Furthermore, that text will have a much different meaning according to the context in which it is read, and this includes the time period. By this argument, an essay by Francis Bacon cannot but have a different message for modern readers than it had for readers of Bacon's own epoch.

The dialogism—or influence of one discourse upon the next—occurs at multiple levels. One of the great conceits of language traditionalists is that, in keeping their language pure by prohibiting the influx of foreign words, they might safeguard a national aesthetic and heritage. Bakhtin would argue that because today's languages have far more contact with each other than ever before, all languages are influenced by "alien" tongues, contaminated by other dialects, foreign words, and concepts. All languages are polyglot and in a sense all language users speak multiple languages.

Even if it were possible to speak "one" language, the speakers of any language are familiar with a variety of different speech genres. They use different registers: writing an academic paper, speaking to colleagues, writing a letter to a close friend, speaking with close friends. They borrow words, phrases, and discourses from other genres—an academic paper may be peppered with French, a conversation with a friend may borrow from "baseballese" for its metaphors—but they also quote directly and indirectly; they appropriate the discourses of other people, friends, acquaintances, lecturers, television personalities, and film characters as they talk or write.

Whatever the language or register, speakers also perpetually shape their discourse for the listener, whether real or imagined. All discourse, Bakhtin writes, "provokes an answer, anticipates it and structures itself in the answer's direction" (1981, 280). This, Bakhtin argues, results in a kind of tension.

> [A]ny concrete discourse (utterance) finds the object at which it was directed already as it were overlain with qualifications, open to dispute, charged with value, already enveloped in an obscuring mist—or, on the contrary, by the "light" of alien words that have already been spoken about it. It is entangled, shot through with shared thoughts, points of voice, alien values, judgments and accents. The word, directed toward its object, enters a dialogically agitated and tension-filled environment of alien words, value judgments and accents, weaves in and out of complex interrelationships, merges with some, recoils from others, intersects with yet a third group: and all of this may crucially shape

> discourse, may leave a trace in all its semantic layers, may complicate
> its expression and influence its entire stylistic profile. (1981, 276)

A dyadic conversation is not merely a situation wherein two speakers work at coming to an understanding, but rather those speakers bring together a plurality of speakers whose words the interlocutors have heard and read, spoken or written; all need to be dealt with, negotiated, used, twisted, and reshaped as they evolve into understandings. Understanding occurs when the speaker "breaks through the alien conceptual horizon of the listener, constructs his own utterance on alien territory, against his, the listener's, apperceptive background" (282).

Bakhtin's theory of understanding is dependent upon the existence of a force opposing the dialogic "realities of heteroglossia" as described here. This force, which Bakhtin calls "centripetal," is the weaker of the two forces and posits a fixed and unitary language that exists only in essence but that provides a basis from which to resist the "centrifugal" and disruptive forces of heteroglossia (271). The centripetal force is necessary to explain how discourse can cohere and make sense in a world where the natural dynamic of language is agitatedly kinetic.

Breaking Apart Voice in Bakhtin

The literal voice—the one we use to speak—is temporally limited, having an audible starting point, endpoint, and sound contours, implying boundedness and materiality and conferring those same characteristics to whatever it is linked to metaphorically. In narratology (see Chapter 1), a specific narrative tone means that a narrative has a sound, rhythm, or style that can be identified and located, as a result of both its consistency and cohesion. In writing instruction, a coherent way of presenting oneself—whether it be one's authentic self or one of the many selves that are constructed for rhetorical purposes—implies not only an identifiability and a locatability but also a certain fixity that enables a reader or critic to identify or locate. If, however, we conceive of discourse in Bakhtinian terms, as always a collection of discourses, styles, and meanings, this concept of a fixed and cohesive discourse becomes troublesome. The perceived cohesiveness comes as a result of a reader's or writer's determination to make sense, to see unity; belief in centripetal force is at the heart of the necessary complicity between reader and writer, who must both believe that texts are the results of specific intentions that will be clearly communicated and understood. In other words, the writer has intentions (of conveying something, arguing a point, revealing a revery); the reader assumes—linguists refer to this as *speech act theory*—that the writer has the intention of conveying something and looks for an intention, maybe even creates it. Interlocutors, when they consider the communication as successful, believe that they understand all that is intended.

But given the stronger centrifugal or disruptive forces that proliferate meaning and sense, could there still be such a thing as a consistent voice? Writers certainly have some control in their selections of linguistic patterns, such as a preponderance of latinate vocabulary, colloquialisms, or periodic sentences. But these patterns themselves are collocations of other patterns (of words or discourses), and even if we accord the writer the power of language selection, supervision, and management—assuming that a person is ever entirely free to select the language she wants—ultimately writing down words and sentences cannot free written language from the influence of previous uses and histories. The reader encounters these words and sentences embedded in an always new context (the novel or essay or poem), where he tries to endow them with sense. In fact, as the reader attempts to do this, he accords each word or phrase with an "influx of sense," incorporating them into the already lively realm of his inner speech. Volosinov, a colleague of Bakhtin, explains.

> Everything vital in the evaluative reception of another's utterance, everything of any ideological value, is expressed in the material of inner speech. After all, it is not a mute, wordless creature that receives such an utterance, but a human being full of inner words. All his experiences—his so-called apperceptive background—exist encoded in his inner speech, and only to that extent do they come into contact with speech received from the outside. (1973, 118)

But as we have seen with Vygotsky, this inner speech consists of words and phrases that are submerged in sense as a result of the social aspect of linguistic interaction; it cannot be helped. Discourse is not a private thing, and control is, in many ways, as illusory as presence. Both, however, may be necessary fictions.

In some ways, voice—as in multiple, interacting, dialogic voices—seems a very appropriate metaphor to portray the movement of heteroglossia. Bakhtin, however, uses the term sparingly. He refers to heteroglossia in the novel as "constitut[ing] a special type of *double-voiced discourse*" (324) in the way the novel incorporates the speech of others to express an author's intentions, albeit it a "refracted way." Even so, Michael Holquist's inclusion of voice in his glossary to *The Dialogic Imagination* indicates that voice is a key term for Bakhtin. Holquist defines voice as "the speaking personality, the speaking consciousness. A voice always has a will or desire behind it, its own timbre and overtones" (434). Unfortunately this explanation raises more difficulties than it resolves, for while the speaking personality may have a will or desire behind it, it is also plural or multiple because it uses and is therefore created by language. Volosinov:

> The inner subjective personality with its own self-awareness does not exist as a material fact, usable as a basis for causal explanation, but it exists as an ideologeme . . . that is vague and fluid in character. . . . Language lights up the inner personality and its consciousness; language creates them and endows them with intricacy and profundity— and it does not work the other way. . . . The generation of the inner consciousness will depend upon the generative process of language, in terms, of course, of language's grammatical and concrete ideological structure. (1973, 152–153)[2]

If personality is created or elucidated by language, and language is polyglossic, then the concept of voice in most of its instantiations can only exist in its perpetual disintegration and reconstruction. It must continually fail at being unitary, coherent, and consistent because within one's voice are always the refractions of the voices of others, themselves heteroglossic. Bakhtin may have sensed this problem, relying more on terms like *word, discourse, language,* and *heteroglossia* than on *voice*. When he does use it—and this seems to be one of the inconsistencies in *The Dialogic Imagination*—it is to describe the individual voices that inhabit the multivoiced realm of the novel (see 263).

Another of the inconsistencies in Bakhtin's work is his exclusion of poetry from the dialogic world of language. He argues that among all the discourse genres, only poetic language is unitary, as poets purposely work to foreclose on the dialogic reverberation(s) that characterize the novel and other genres. Poetry may occasionally participate in heteroglossia, but "[e]ven when speaking of alien things, the poet speaks in his own language" (287), crafting it to silence the influx of sense from other settings. The poet achieves poetic status only "insofar as he accepts the idea of a unitary and singular language and a unitary, monologically sealed-off utterance" (296) that "forgets its previous life in any other contexts" (297), and creates a unique and unified work, distinguished by its univocality. Although the distinctions are dubious, the difference between poetry and the novel seem to have to do with authorial intentions; the novelist's goal is to engage and incorporate other discourses, giving them free play, while the poet seeks to subsume or harness other discourses within the unifying framework of his own poetic purpose. In reality, the distinctions between novelists and poets, and between novels and poems do not consistently organize themselves along polyvocal and univocal lines. T. S. Eliot's modernist poems, for example, seem to revel in the multiple, fragmented voices from other sources. Moreover, in separating poetry out from the rest of discourse, Bakhtin reinforces two of the modern problems with voice. First, he promotes, perhaps inadvertently, the romantic notion of the poet who works alone to create a private and unitary language. And second, he implies that the poet's work is somehow magical in that she can produce something that other writers cannot, given the difficulty of silencing heteroglossia. Perhaps he is suggesting that unitary language cannot be fashioned by the average writer, that it requires literary genius, another notion celebrated by many Romantic poets.

Bakhtin himself is suspicious of this kind of magical thinking. The recognition that language is heteroglossic, he argues, results in the destruction of "magical" or "mythological" thinking that fuses stable, coherent—even monolithic—language systems with thought, particularly ideological thought (368–369). Magical thinking limits linguistic flexibility, applicability, and hence, expressiveness. When magical thinking ceases, then it becomes possible to believe in

> an artistically complete image of a characteristic human way of sensing and seeing the world. Language, no longer conceived as a sacrosanct and solitary embodiment of meaning and truth, becomes merely one of many possible ways to hypothesize meaning. (370)

Distinctly reminiscent of Derrida's critique of the transcendental signifier, this passage illustrates an important connection between deconstruction and heteroglossia—or between the philosophy of language and the sociology of language—and suggests that the trend toward dialogic perspectives is one that has come at us from many different directions.

Still, the issue of a textual persona is not entirely resolved, for although it may be possible to acknowledge the centrifugal, kinetic, multiform quality of language, many theorists still contend that most readers strive to comprehend what they read as being controlled by a governing persona.

The Foucauldian Ego

The illusion of the controlling persona may be best handled by Foucault, who explores different ways of conceiving this governing persona by tackling the problem of authorship from the perspective of the writer or the writing "ego." As I suggested earlier, the actual presence of the speaker in an oral conversation has an enormous effect on the creation of a speaking persona; in oral speech acts, the "speaking ego"—as Foucault might call it—is literally present at the scene. In writing, there is no literal author present, making it possible to perceive more readily how the language an individual speaks is not the language of an individual ego but of what Foucault calls a "plurality of egos" (1977, 130). Although texts may provide many indications that they are the product of a single ego—the use of an author's name on the title page, first-person personal pronoun reference, allusions to the author's personal world and world knowledge—this ego is never fixed or situated in a single entity.

Foucault exemplifies this argument with a mathematical treatise. The author/ego who sets up the parameters of a project in the beginning of the treatise—giving the reasons why it has been written and any pertinent background details—is a much different ego from the one who is engaged in the project and its discussion. This ego, in turn, differs from the one who sets about evaluating the project and analyzing the results. Foucault explains:

> We are not dealing with a system of dependencies where a first and essential use of the "I" is reduplicated, as a kind of fiction, by the other two. On the contrary, the "author-function" in such discourses operates so as to effect the simultaneous dispersion of the three egos. (130)

By the same token, an author/ego who writes the preface to a book will be different from the author/ego of the body of the book. Other egos manifest themselves in the creation of such genre conventions as chapters and their shape, prologues, subheadings, indices, and so on. These particular generic structures are physical; they are visual organizational conventions as well as textual ones, shaping an "author" that is multiform rather than unitary. Even the idea of a consistent person is improbable, since it will always shift according to its task (and context, etc.). The actual voices that speakers use are physical and organizational tools also, in the sense that these oral voices develop the character of the "author" through the speakers' physical mannerisms and qualities and their deployment of language (including intonation, inflection, and stress). But as we have hopefully come to recognize, they represent the same kind of ongoing fluctuation and transformation as the written authorial character.

Voice and the Dynamics of Power

Does all discourse, then, lack the kind of control that has traditionally been ascribed to well-written texts? Are there not accepted organizing principles that govern discourses despite the fact that the discourses themselves are intrinsically multiple, dialogic, and mutable? Discourse, in fact, is rarely looked upon as anarchic or cacophonous, as the merging of a "plurality of egos" into a text (including oral and written "texts"). Most texts are, more often than not, considered coherent and cohesive, conveying some sort of central meaning or "main point," although precisely what that meaning entails is always open to question. Even conversation, which because of processing constraints lacks the kind of control a written (and edited) text has, is rarely characterized as aimless, meandering chat; ultimately there seems to be a point or series of points the speaker intends to convey, whether it be to persuade the listener of some longstanding theory, hold forth on an idea or position, or make personal contact in order to reinforce a relationship. Usually the listener's goal—consciously or unconsciously—is to determine what this point is, to believe it, refute it, dismiss it, or remain indifferent to it.

One way of considering how this coherence is achieved is to look at a stretch of discourse as "managed" discourse. We might, then, appraise how the multiple discourses (which includes quoted material) that a writer incorporates into a text threaten to usurp the initiating writer (author) and how, or if, that writer achieves control. The initiating writer has potentially the greatest power because it is she who shapes the discourses of others in her text, violating the integrity of those discourses, altering the way they are read and understood by establishing her own context; the characters' dialogue, the directly and indirectly quoted language, the alternative points of view are all presented on her terms.

A brief glance at some examples of academic prose illustrates how this management of discourses might work. In the first example, Frederic Jameson (1981), known for his insightful control over difficult material (or "discourses"), makes some rhetorically astute moves in the opening chapter of *The Political Unconscious*, managing his text in ways that ostensibly give him control. In the development of his theme, that literature is a socially symbolic act, he incorporates long quotations to set up his argument. One from Althusser spans one and a half pages, and in that space, one could argue that the dominant perspective becomes that of Althusser, that Jameson allows Althusser's discourse at all levels—language, ideas, and rhetorical patterns—to supersede his own. The governing context, however, has been created by Jameson, so that what he allows Althusser to say is also now Jameson's, used—and this applies in the pejorative sense as well—and slanted to the point Jameson wants to make. Despite this, the discourse in this chapter is not all under Jameson's control; one might also call it *double-voiced*, to use a Bakhtinian term, and in the hands of a less skilled writer, could conceivably move out of his control. Jameson uses Althusser to make the point he wants, so he gives Althusser the floor and the credit, as convention dictates, and the temporary ownership of the page(s).

A considerable amount of work has been done on "reported speech" (Bakhtin, Volosinov) and the "active relation" between that speech and the surrounding context. Volosinov, for example, insists that "[t]he reporting context strives to break down the self-contained compactness of the reported speech, to resolve it, to obliterate its boundaries" (155).

But while it is widely assumed—both in popular uses in the news media as well as in its use in academic circles—that quoted speech is changed substantially by the narrating framework, the degree to which the narrating framework is transformed by the reported speech is barely acknowledged. If the boundaries are "obliterated," one should then assume—in dialogic fashion—that all participating discourses are altered.

Jameson also includes a discussion and quotation from Gilles Deleuze and Felix Guattari's *Anti-Oedipus* that he presents as one example of an alternative to traditional interpretive methods. Since Jameson wants to present his own method of interpretation, he apparently does not want to allow Deleuze and Guattari's discourses to occupy much space in his text. In fact, he summarizes their argument in a footnote (23), in a sense both registering and dispensing with it, a move that—one could argue—reaffirms his own "voice" and undermines theirs, reducing them in his text. He cites a great many writers and thinkers over the course of the book, and the degree to which their perspectives and discourses become subsumed within his own is related to how they are allowed to speak, that is, how much of the space on the page is given over to their discourses or how much authority they are granted in the discussion. What Jameson offers here is, at one level, a demonstration of rhetorical power, the skillful inclusion of other discourses to manage and use them.

But this approach to a stylistic analysis of Jameson does much to reinforce the conceptions of voice that I have been attempting to discredit. In fact, this stylistic analysis reveals a text that is double-voiced instead of multivoiced, and does not live up to the kind of multileveled heteroglossia that is so persuasive in Bakhtin's dialogism. Instead of neatly integrated, managed discourses, I believe that what we're really hearing—if hearing is what we do when we read—is a highly populated discourse, a kind of organized cacophony with multiple articulations, brought together not only by Jameson but by Althusser and *his* highly populated discourse, and then by Deleuze and Guattari, fashioned to *mix* with varying conceptions of Marxism, French philosophy, and multiple strands in literary theory, as well as to *conflict* with them—influenced finally by the intentions and goals of the readers of *The Political Unconscious*. Jameson's text changes Althusser's and Deleuze and Guattari's just as they change Jameson's. *The Political Unconscious* is, then, not a unified text because it cannot be. As I have suggested earlier, unity is an illusion, necessary only to traditional conceptions of "making sense." The book is replete with ideas, collocations, conflicts, and dialogic tensions that can never be resolved in any permanent way. Coherence is derived from the readers' and writers' presuppositions of coinciding intentions—the reader assumes that Jameson has certain goals and ideas in mind, and Jameson assumes that the same is true of the reader, although the possibility of these goals squarely coinciding is slim to none. The effort at coordinating intentions, however, is what induces Jameson to employ a broad range of textual conventions such as chapters and chapter headings, certain kinds of paragraphing strategies, logical connectors, and other cuing devices to provide the necessary illusion of control. And these are indeed necessary if what readers are looking for is a point. But looking for a point tends to devalue the other "experiences" and learning in the reading of the text, which are no less valid or valuable.

What are these other experiences? If the text is as anarchic as I have suggested here, what, one might ask, could the reader possibly learn from it? The answer is a complicated one. A reader may or may not come away with the sense of having been persuaded of one argument, but will have followed (or even failed to follow) the twistings and turnings of a spectrum of different arguments; she will have experienced the influence of contexts and learned about their discursive presentation. Moreover, she will have encountered a new lexicon, not necessarily consisting of new words, but of new "senses" of known words as they are enmeshed in syntactical constructions that are different from those she might have previously encountered. Certainly she could, in fine academic fashion, summarize Jameson's main theme that literature is a socially symbolic act—like I did on page 75. It is there, made plain by Jameson's cues—and she can hold this in mind as she reads, following the logic she finds, accumulating evidence provided both by the text and from her own world knowledge, substantiating her supposition that this book has a *main point* and that it is indeed being pursued. But in reading through even the first chapter she has learned vastly more about, for example, language play, eroding control, manipulation, and ambiguity. Reading for a main point and searching for textual unity that works toward that point is what makes voice possible.

Anthologies provide a different kind of example. Hazard Adams's well-known anthology of literary theory, *Critical Theory Since Plato*, contains more than a hundred entries from critical theorists. He provides a general introduction and then introduces each entry, summarizing its thesis or key points and including brief information about its author and his or her place in history. Through this, it might be argued, we get a sense of Adams' own voice, why he made the selections he did—both in terms of the choice of writers included and choice of excerpts from their work—and his own position, proclivities, and style, especially if we consider such elements as the length of excerpt, method of introduction, footnoting, and bibliographic entries as elements of style. The impact of this volume is like no other—hence, the argument that this volume bears the imprint of a persona, even if, in this case, it is created editorially. An editor contributes to the "writing" (in a large sense) of the book.

However, the discourses that Adams includes specifically threaten one another, jeopardizing the hegemony that each exerts as it is read or studied or revoiced; the presence of William Blake and Kenneth Burke in the volume changes the other selections. The ideas each excerpt introduces, the language that each uses to discuss ideas, and the style that characterizes each text all shape the general context of the passages on critical theory that are to follow and those that precede. The fact, for example, that Plato's *Ion* is included and that Plato's *Phaedrus* is not, alters the conception of Aristotle's *Poetics,* the next selection; the *Poetics* is "entangled, shot through with shared thoughts, points of view, alien values, judgments and accents" (Bakhtin, cited earlier) that are drawn at least in part from the surrounding context.

One could argue that we can hear the voice of Adams in his overall selection of excerpts, and the individual voices of the writers that he has elected to include, and that this creates a text in which voices can be understood as discrete as well as multivoiced. But, again, this accords an almost monolithic integrity to the writers' voices and limits us to a reading that insists upon certain boundaries between voices. If it is possible to avoid looking for autonomous voices—and I'm not sure it is, given the degree to which voice is embedded in our cultural consciousness—then we might instead explore actions and reactions, much as a chemist might, and come to ongoing (versus static or fixed) understandings of how language and ideas collude, collide, deteriorate, and regenerate. We'd certainly approach our reading with different kinds of expectations and come away with a different kind of experiences.

If we accept a Bakhtinian model of discourse, then all texts are, in a sense, "anthologized," and the writer is never the "actual writer." Even if the writer is in some sense a textual manager, what the reader in fact encounters are attempts to manage other discourses, which, in turn, struggle with one other, each impinging dialogically upon the integrity of the rest. And integrity can only be a temporary thing.

Intellectual Property—A Pragmatic Example

There are numerous implications for understanding texts in the ways I have described here. One of the most problematic of these has to do with ownership, plagiarism, and intellectual property. The work done in this area has been extensive (see, for example, Mallon 1989; Lunsford and Ede 1990; Woodmansee and Jaszi 1994), and I have no intention of rehearsing the central arguments here. Instead I want to demonstrate the problem and suggest a way of looking at intellectual property that seeks to make voice less of a featured player.

Accusations of plagiarism and the concomitant intellectual dishonesty frequently make national news. In the past ten years, complaints have been levied against Martin Luther King, Jr., Bruno Bettelheim, historian Stephen Oates, William Safire, and countless other nationally known figures. One of the reasons for the public indignation and hence, publicity, has to do with the kinds of values we hold as a society that also help sustain voice as a metaphor.

Let's consider Bettelheim's case. Bettelheim is a major figure in child psychology, well known to those in fields that range from psychiatry to child development. His status in those fields is a result not only of what Bettelheim has thought, discussed, and written, but of how his ideas fit with existing thoughts, discussions, and writings. In other words, the Bettelheim persona has been created as much by his field as by his personal accomplishments; his personal accomplishments, if you will, only have meaning against the achievements of his field. But consider a sample of his "crime." The following is from Bettelheim's *The Uses of Enchantment* (1976):

> One must never "explain" to the child the meaning of fairy tales. However, the narrator's understanding of the fairy tale's message to the child's preconscious mind is important. . . . It furthers the adult's sensitivity to selection of those stories which are most appropriate to the child's state of development and to the specific psychological difficulties he is confronted with at the moment.

He is accused of plagiarizing that passage from Julius E. Heuscher, who, in 1963, wrote:

> While one must never "explain" the fairy tales to the child, the narrator's understanding of their meaning is very important. It furthers the sensitivity for selecting those stories which are most appropriate in various phases of children's development and for stressing those themes which may be therapeutic for specific psychological difficulties.

The similarities between the passages are unsettling because they indicate that Bettelheim's work was not original and that he was taking credit for work done by someone else. But when the allegedly plagiarized passages were shown to Heuscher, he seemed a bit perplexed.

> We all plagiarize. I plagiarize. Many times I am not sure whether it came out of my brain or if it came from somewhere else. I'm only happy that I would have influenced Bruno Bettelheim. I did not always agree with him. But that does not matter. Poor Bruno Bettelheim. I would not want to disturb his eternal sleep for this. (*Los Angeles Times*, Feb. 7, 1991, Sect. A28)

Apparently, in an environment where ideas and words are perceived to flow freely, and knowledge and discourses are shared, it seemed to make little sense to Heuscher to mark off boundaries between one person's words or voice and another's—and for that matter, to measure one person's contribution against another's—especially when it is often impossible to tell what came from whom. Giving credit where credit is due is a precept belonging to a value system that is deeply embedded in our individualistic, capitalist culture. One's work is a commodity, and it means things in terms of personal and professional advancement, especially when financial gain in based on one's achievement. Furthermore, if writing is regarded as the outpouring of one's authentic inner self, then for someone else to appropriate that writing under her own name or any name other than the original is not just forgery; it is equivalent to doing violence to another's self, a violation of considerable proportions.

If, however, we believe that the boundaries between the individual and the social world are always blurred, especially in language acts, then using the language of another person is a fact of life; it's the way language works.

Interestingly, prevailing conceptions of plagiarism in academia are reminiscent of what has been frequently described as "current-traditional" rhetoric. The concept, for example, that there is a stable one-to-one correspondence between thought and the language that expresses that thought permits a commodification of language that facilitates ownership. Language, of course, has to be owned before it can be stolen.

Clearly, many accusations of plagiarism go well beyond intellectual property issues. In the cases of King and Bettelheim, the charges may have been designed to discredit not only the man and his work, but his race, his beliefs, his politics, or his other affiliations. It is ironic that Bettelheim's chief accuser, Alan Dundes, is an expert on folklore, the literature of an oral culture, which if owned at all, belongs to whole cultures rather than individuals.

Should ownership of voice be an issue? Does power in discourse come from a particular and idiosyncratic voice or from the management and shaping of disparate (and often conflicting) discourses to function in particular ways for particular audiences and situations? The extraordinary power King had as a public speaker and writer are not truly his. King is the product of a very rich evangelical background that he drew upon to touch chords in his audience's religious and spiritual experiences; this is part of his power. The effectiveness of his work is not reduced because it is not the original creation of a single person. In fact, I would argue that it is greatly enhanced because the power has to do with chemistry: interrelated and probably infinite sets of actions and reactions.

The fact that plagiarism does not conform to current popular theoretical conceptions of language obviously doesn't mean we should tell our students to stop worrying about stealing term papers off the World Wide Web or to relax when a colleague publishes an article that we wrote five years ago. However, rather than relying on a paradigm that also underlies the voice metaphor to explain why uncredited borrowing is unethical, it seems more productive to consider plagiarism as a rhetorical problem, one that involves not just the writer and the writing but the audience, context, and nature of the medium. It might be more worthwhile, for example, to explain to students how our rules about plagiarism have to do with conventions, which can result in censure by an audience if disregarded or defied, whether they are based on outdated concepts or not. Exploring the assumptions about language that makes plagiarism possible, including the contradictions inherent in a course that combines collaborative writing projects and traditional grading systems based on individual achievement, can result in real learning (messy and often ambiguous) rather than information transmission.

However we handle problems of intellectual property and unethical borrowing, there are no easy answers, primarily because the issues rest on assumptions that are deeply embedded in our collective psyches. The last two chapters of this book, however, suggest alternatives to the voice metaphor that open up these issues to possibility and potential.

Notes

1. See Erving Goffman, *The Presentation of Self in Everyday Life* (New York: Doubleday, 1959), for a more detailed discussion of "face."

2. Note that for both Bakhtin and Volosinov, ideologies are simply idea systems, and ideologemes are utterances that reveal ideology.

Chapter 5

Voicing and Revoicing

Every reproduction, every poetic recitation, every theatrical performance—however great the performers may be—only succeeds in communicating a genuine artistic experience of the work itself if with our inner ear we hear something quite different from what actually takes place in front of us. The constituent elements with which we construct the work are not provided by the reproduction, the presentation, or the theatrical performance as such, but by the work that has been raised to ideality in our inner ear. Anyone who knows a poem particularly well has experienced this. (Gadamer, *The Relevance of the Beautiful,* 44)

Despite my determined protestations against using voice in talking about writing or reading, this *is* a book about voice as much as it is a criticism. To honor that, this chapter does a preliminary about-face, presenting some evidence as to the effectiveness of considering voice in specific instances and in specific contexts. In what may be an impossible task because I believe language is inherently metaphorical, I want to detach the literal voice from the metaphorical one, strip it of some of its entailments and trappings, and consider how the voice participates in composing and reading. While this turn may be a bit unorthodox for a theoretical book such as this, it is also an attempt to keep the already large scope of this book rooted in the serviceable and functional.

In the epigraph, Hans-Georg Gadamer maintains that the aesthetic experience of drama and poetic recitation is constructed in the inner ear of the audience. In this chapter, I would like to use Gadamer's statement as a point of departure for an investigation of the "inner ear." In broadening Gadamer's application to include not only "performed" texts (drama and recited poetry) but all texts, I will pursue the concept of "voicing" by examining evidence for the material existence of voice as it manifests itself in reading. I will move from there to suggest how much of what readers do with texts has to do with visual understanding as well as aural, arguing that the relationship between the two is at times cooperative and at other times exclusionary.

One of the problems with "authentic voice" pedagogy is that it has tended to place primary emphasis on the site of textual production, that is, with the writer. In other words (and as we have seen in earlier chapters), voice has tended to be a cornerstone for expressivist pedagogies. More recently, theorists (see, for example, Elbow 1994; Farmer 1995; Ritchie 1989) have adapted voice in an effort to make it a viable metaphor in a discipline that privileges social and cultural perspectives of language over the merely expressivist. In the course of this chapter, I will appear to realign voice with the dialogics of response that many of these theorists advocate, but will ultimately suggest that the only useful application of voice may stem from an understanding of how the literal voice operates in reading.

A brief look at the treatment and study of literal voice serves to contextualize a discussion that will help formulate the value to pedagogy of the revoicing concept.

Vocal Gesturing

There has been a great deal of study of the sound of language in the fields of phonetics and phonology, but relatively little examination of how characteristics of the physical speaking voice influence meaning. Because oratory was a more prominent field of study and inquiry for classical rhetoricians than writing, voice quality was one of the important elements that marked a good orator. Both Greek and Roman texts about rhetoric pay attention to voice timbre, vocal clarity (enunciation), pronunciation, and intonation. Quintilian, as I noted earlier, had high regard for "the living voice," maintaining that "it feeds the mind more nutritiously" than reading (*Institutio oratoria* Book I, 28–29) and is more lively, more forceful, than writing.

Concern about the importance of vocal gesturing also comes from the theatrical arts. In Renaissance texts about acting, especially among English dramatists of the sixteenth century and the Italian tradition of *commedia dell'arte*, there was a shift away from highly stylized methods of dramatic performance that characterized the classicists and academicians and toward a more natural style of acting.[1] Improvisation was

an acceptable dramatic form and dramatists such as Pietro Maria Cec-
chini and Andrea Perrucci discussed in their writings ways in which
actors can use language, voice, and gesture to appear both natural and
entertaining. Recommendations to actors from this period indicate an
emerging semiology that emphasized the importance of gesture—
physical and vocal—and its strong connection to the emotion to be
conveyed. In his *Dialogues on State Affairs* ([1556–1565] 1970), Leoni di
Somi wrote that "the actor's movements are of so great importance that
perhaps the power of words is not more than the power of gesture" (48).

Later, in the seventeenth-century English theater, Colley Cibber
continued the trend of the Italians, speaking admiringly of actor Thomas
Betterton, who possessed such extraordinary vocal genius that

> it shone out in every speech and motion of him. . . . [V]oice, and per-
> son, are such necessary supports of [genius], that, by the multitude
> they have been preferred to genius itself. . . . Betterton had a voice of
> that kind which gave more spirit to terror than to the softer passions;
> of more strength than melody. ([1556–1565] 1970, 107)

Outside the theater, Francis Bacon set in motion a trend that dealt
with perfecting a scientific approach for pronunciation and gesture, resulting in works such as John Bulwer's *Chirologia* (1644), an illustrated
manual of physical gesture for public speakers. Bulwer advises, for example, that "[t]o apply the hand passionately to the head is a sign of *an-
guish, sorrow, grief, impatiency* and *lamentation* used also by those who
accuse or *justify* themselves" (71). In the eighteenth century, John Walker
and Thomas Sheridan wrote dictionaries that were designed to provide
a guide for the oral delivery of written texts, demonstrating an increased
emphasis on pronunciation and elocution that would last until rhetoric
waned in importance as a field of study in the nineteenth century.

Nonetheless, the study of the actual physical performance of discourse has been only a peripheral concern, both in the history of rhetoric and in the more modern field of linguistics. One reason for this, in
linguistics at least, may stem from the influence of the Saussurian distinction between *langue* and *parole*. Early linguistics (late nineteenth
and early twentieth century) was considered a "science" of language
and occupied itself with *langue,* or a person's underlying knowledge of
language, a system separate from actual speech or *parole*. This underlying system could be analyzed according to its structure and system-
atized according to rule-governed formulae, which, because *langue*
was bracketed off from actual speech, could make accurate and consistent predictions, as scientific models should. This distinction is perpetuated in Noam Chomsky's influential competence/performance model
in which competence can be roughly linked to *langue* and performance

to *parole*. Chomsky has argued that because performance is filled with the kinds of disfluencies and speaker errors that muddy the linguistic output, the language that speakers actually use is often a bastardized version of their language competence. Although performance is not necessarily rejected by Chomsky as a legitimate object of study, more attention and prestige has been accorded to competence.

In recent years, as sociolinguistics has taken hold as a viable field of study, work has been done that appears more performance-oriented. William Labov's (1984) study of phonological variation in the speech of New Yorkers as a marker of class and gender affiliation is one example. In Norwich, England, Peter Trudgill (1974) traced phonological variables across social classes. These and other studies are aimed at describing and defining speech communities and concern themselves with competence in the sense of social communicative competence. Very few studies, however—perhaps because the object of study oscillates toward the unpredictable and highly unstable performance end of the competence/performance model—have dealt with what might be regarded as secondary language features, such as intonation, pitch, stress, and loudness as they operate as performatives and affect meaning. Among the notable exceptions are Thomas Kochman's (1981) studies of Black English in the inner cities, which treat black prosody and the problems it creates in communication with white communities. Most studies, however, fail to come to terms with how these vocal features might affect meaning in oral conversations.

Another reason for this lack is that precisely how the "voiced" qualities of language work is difficult to assess; it is not easy to describe with precision what is communicated by the ways in which the words are voiced and by acoustical variations. Stress placed on a particular word in a sentence, a clipped syllable, a pause, rising or falling pitch, all potentially shape meaning. But how is this achieved? Consider the following sentence:

The counterattack this time is against the Longhorn beetle.

Some of the stress is dictated by the grammatical construction. For example, *this* would in most cases be accented more than *time* because of its adjectival position before *time* and as the first word after the subject of the sentence. But many of the other choices of stress, glide, syllable and word accent, vowel quality, and pitch jump are up to the speaker, her emotional state, her framing of the context, and the desired focus. If, for example, *Longhorn* were stressed, a distinction would be made between that kind of fruit fly and another. *Longhorn* becomes a focus. If *beetle* were stressed, the speaker is distinguishing between *beetle* and something else "longhorned." What is stressed is often new information.

If *counterattack* were stressed, resulting in a diminishment of *this time,* some special attention to the type or quality of the attack might be implied. And these are only a very limited subset of the intonational possibilities of this sentence. Boredom, frustration, anger, jubilation may result in quite different intonational variations with only minimal regard for what its grammatical structure might suggest.

In addition to these options, there are other ways to translate vocal gesturing into writing. An italicized word can be read as loudness, stress, staccato, and so on. Punctuation can indicate pauses (commas), elevated pitch (exclamation marks), or rising intonation (question marks). But these qualities often seem arbitrary and irregular partly because they do not appear to be systematic. One of the reasons for this lack of systematicity may have to do with the relationship between language and emotion and the difficulty of accurately categorizing emotional states. In *Intonation and Its Parts,* Dwight Bolinger (1986) examines how pitch, accent, and intonation figure in spoken discourse and explains how the intonation patterns we use are drawn both from the grammatical structure of a language and the emotional status or directives of a speaker.

> Though intonation is indispensable to grammar, the grammatical functions of intonation are secondary to the emotional ones; speakers feel differently about what they say and the feelings manifest themselves in pitch changes that serve as clues. One proof of the emotional rather than the logical nature of intonation—its symptomatic more than symbolic character—is the fact that speakers rarely if ever objectify the choice of an intonation pattern; they do not stop and ask themselves "Which form would be best here for my purpose?" as they frequently do in selecting a word or a grammatical construction. Instead, they identify the feeling they wish to convey, and the intonation is triggered by it. They may make mistakes and have to correct themselves—even automatic choices may occasionally be off target—but the correction will be just as unreflecting as the original choice. (27)

Because to communicate a feeling relates strongly to a speaker's intention, it would seem that intonational choices are not so unreflecting and prone to the vagaries of trial-and-error as Bolinger suggests. Intentions are always tempered by the same aspects of context that influence both grammatical and lexical choices,[2] but Bolinger may be correct in assuming that choices based on emotion may be more deeply buried in one's subconscious and therefore not as subject to rational choice.

Speech is rarely if ever spoken in monotones. "A monotone," Bolinger writes, "is powerless speech" (74), and it is powerless because in its neutrality, it fails to convey feeling or interest. Although they are extraordinarily rare in speech, "neutral sentences" merely "tell";

they don't say much else about what can be played up or played down (99–100). If, for example, a speaker says the following sentence aloud, giving each syllable, insofar as possible, the same accent and pitch, she states a proposition but strips it of important markers of attitude and intention.

He was simply following directions.

This, of course, is not what listeners expect from speech. Rather, they look for clues as to the emotional intent of the speaker. The ability to read these clues, Bolinger argues, is critical to a person's survival in the world, helping listeners perceive a speaker's anger, irony, double meaning, jokes, sensitivity, and playfulness. Errors in reading intonational signs result in problems of awkwardness, embarrassment, or worse.

Bolinger's explanation of monotone parallels Elbow's notion of "voiceless prose" and Macrorie's "Engfish." Bolinger's study suggests that the problem with voiceless prose is that it is starkly propositional; prose with voice, like speech with intonation, supposedly contains an abundance of meaning.

> Though it has been specialized, symptomatic communication of this sort [changes in pitch and voice quality] is PRESENTATIVE rather then REPRESENTATIVE. In this respect, it differs from those communicative acts whose meaning-carriers bear no natural relationship to their meanings—the distinctive sounds ([t] of *time,* [l] of *lime*), the arbitrary words (why are cats called *cats?*), and the fossilized arrangements (*Dogs bite cats, Cats bite dogs*). Intonation is EXPRESSIVE, and, to some degree at least, spontaneous. (195)

Spontaneity—or the effect of spontaneity—achieved through intonation or its equivalents in written language (active voice, first-person reference, emotional language, personal attitude) is, apparently, what makes language powerful.

My goal here, however, is not to systematize or to develop a taxonomy of intonation and its parts but rather to suggest that it may be some kind of intonational equivalent that voice proponents would like to see translated into the language of texts. Because current textual criticism is inclined to be more reader-focused, attempting to avoid the intentional fallacy through interpretive strategies such as reader-response and interpretive communities, the kinds of powerful and dynamic effects that the speaker creates in spoken language is not the same for a writer; the effects are not the creation of the writer or even a mediation between the writer and reader. They are ultimately something the reader does. Thus, I want to shift the focus of this discussion to the act of reading as revoicing, framing it as an intonation-giving activity.

The Literal Voice in Reading

Before beginning my discussion of reading, I would like to briefly point to a linguistic theory in speech perception that provides a useful analog to the concept of reader-as-revoicer. In the 1960s and early 1970s, a number of linguists (Halle and Stevens 1962; Liberman, Cooper, Shankweiler, and Studdert-Kennedy 1967; Stevens 1960; Stevens and House 1972) proposed the *motor theory* of speech perception to explain how listeners process speech. They maintained that listeners, when they hear speech, model or articulate that speech via an internal speech synthesizer. In other words, listeners "re-speak" the words they hear as they hear them as part of their language processing. The theory in its strongest version, that is, that listeners literally use their own articulatory system to re-say all incoming words and sentences in order to understand, has largely been rejected for lack of evidence. It would seem likely, however, that a listener may be able to predict the speaker's message and intentions based on firsthand knowledge of what certain varieties of articulation mean.

Historically, readers encountered print in a variety of ways, not always through private reading. Texts were often read aloud to an audience, making reading an oral, public event. Private reading in such cases was considered an oddity, as illustrated by Augustine's account of an episode with St. Ambrose. Apparently, Augustine one day encountered St. Ambrose in his cell reading silently to himself. Because it was customary to read to oneself aloud, this silent reading disturbed Augustine, primarily because he could neither discover nor correct St. Ambrose's interpretation or understanding of the text he was reading (see discussion of Plato in Chapter 2).

Most modern readers encounter print first by seeing it, analyzing or decoding written words via their sense of sight. In private reading, then, readers "re-compose" or reconstitute the already composed language from the chirographic or printed symbols, or, to use a common metaphor, readers obtain meaning—however we define meaning—from the page.

There is considerable evidence that in the process of decoding print, in giving meaning to the words we read, we literally give "voice" to words. Children first learn to read aloud, and this carries over for more advanced readers into subvocalization in silent reading. Numerous studies have indicated that subvocalization occurs even for fluent readers, especially in the reading of difficult passages or in reading where there is outside disturbance or interference (for a review of the relevant literature, see Taylor and Taylor 1983, 210–212). In *Working Memory* (1986), A. Baddeley discusses studies in which he found that when subvocalization, even in adult readers, is prevented by the repetition of nonsense syllables during an act of reading, comprehension and memory for what is read is greatly impaired. Researchers such as Baev (1957), Edfelt (1960), Conrad (1972), Faaborg-Anderson and Edfelt (1958), Hardyck and Petrinovich (1967), McGuigan (1973), and Sokolov (1972) have looked at mental activity in reading and have been able to measure, using an electromyograph (EMG), a significant amount of covert articulation, especially as the reading task increases in difficulty. Williams (1983) also points to evidence that covert articulation occurs during writing tasks as well, the amount of articulation again increasing as the rhetorical task becomes more difficult.

What these studies suggest is that readers convert what they read into an internal representation that is aural, with subvocalization as an important component. One could argue, however, that subvocalization is so minimal in accomplished readers that it has little effect for them. But, in fact, a variety of studies indicate that an aural component may be an important and basic step leading to comprehension. Taylor and Taylor (1983) point to a number of studies that show the degree to which we seem sensitive to the phonetic qualities of written words as we read (214–215). For example, a reader is more likely to recognize misspelled words in a passage if those words are phonetically incompatible (such as "borst" instead of "burst") than if compatible ("hurd" instead of "heard"). Apparently, children develop a phonological store as they learn to read silently to themselves (Conrad 1972) and utilize it to assimilate text. In his studies on the working memory (a variant of the short-term memory), Baddeley hypothesizes the existence of a mechanism he calls the "Articulatory Loop" (in place of a phonological storage mechanism). This loop works like a closed loop on a tape recorder. When readers process text, the Articulatory Loop holds the information in sequence while a cognitive mechanism that Baddeley calls the "Central Executive" organizes the input into meaningful speech sounds, that is, specific names and words, enabling readers to understand a sentence.

In fact, Baddeley believes there are actually two types of phonological storage systems, which he calls the "inner voice" and the "inner ear." In his 1986 studies, he found that though suppression of the articulatory functions prevents visually presented items from being phonologically encoded through the articulation of nonsense syllables or numbers, readers are still capable of making judgments about rhyme and homophony on visually presented words. The *inner voice* uses the articulatory system and is inoperable if articulation or subvocalization is prevented; the *inner ear*, as the receptor, seems to involve imaging that is largely acoustic.

Acoustic imaging seems to play an important role in our sense of clause boundaries and ability to punctate. In "Punctuation and Prosody of Written Language," Wallace Chafe (1988) reports on his study of how adult readers read, looking specifically at how they treat clauses. There is a strong relationship, he argues, between what he calls intonation units, that is, spurts of vocalization that peak and end in a terminal pitch contour, and punctuation units, textual units that are bounded by punctuation. In his study, he asked college-age and older adult readers to read a variety of written passages aloud, which he measured for the length (words per intonation unit and punctuation unit). He found that the oral intonation units were shorter than the written, especially for more academic-style texts. The length of oral intonation units corresponds to the mean length of intonation units in English, which is 5.5 words (Chafe 1980), a length that apparently accommodates the limits of our working memory and our processing and production capabilities (including incidentals such as breathing). By contrast, when the same readers were asked to repunctuate texts from which all forms of punctuation had been removed, they used punctuation in ways that were very faithful to the original. Chafe argues that this shows that reading written discourse aloud seems to conform to speech constraints while repunctuating a text seems to call upon some form of auditory imaging.

Chafe also points out that some writers claim to draw heavily upon their spoken voices in the production of texts. Russell Long, for example, maintains that

> As I write these sentences, even though my lips are not moving, I am quite conscious of the sound the words I am writing would make if they were read aloud. (qtd. in Chafe 1980, 405)

Novelist Eudora Welty ties her writing voice to her "reading voice":

> My own words, when I am at work on a story, I hear too as they go, in the same voice that I hear when I read in books. When I write and the sound of it comes back to my ears, then I act to make my changes. I have always trusted this voice. ([1937] 1965, 13)

What this reveals is that both Long and Welty may have a heightened awareness that the internal mechanism—which they call voice and upon which they rely in composing—is implicitly tied to a reading voice, to what happens in the process of reading. The composer uses his speaking voice to write; the reader then uses a reading voice to "revoice" what she reads. Put another way, the first reader (and, hence, revoicer) of a text is the actual writer of that text in the activity of composing.

While it appears likely, at least in some capacity, that revoicing is called upon when writers write and when readers read, the concept of revoicing that I am proposing is a literal one, entailing the decoding of marks on a page and transferring them to an aural mode. Based on how they interpret the physical signs of print and the contexts, readers give what they read inflection, intonation and phrasing patterns, pitch, stress, and loudness, including pauses. Punctuation such as commas, question and quotation marks, periods, and paragraphing serve as guides to supplement the grammatical patterns of English.

A concrete example helps illustrate possible ways in which readers depend upon an oral articulation in moving from text to meaning. Consider a sample from *Wonderful Life* by Stephen Jay Gould (1989):

> The greatest bit of "field work," as we shall see, occurred in Washington during the spring of 1973, when Whittington's brilliant and eclectic student Simon Conway Morris made a systematic search through *all* the drawers of Walcott's specimens, consciously looking for oddities because he had grasped the germ of the key insight about Burgess disparity. (80)

Words are set apart by quotation marks and italics, and commas mark potential pauses or parentheticals ("as we shall see") and the passage ends with a sentence-final period. These conventions serve as cues for how the passage might be revoiced. Some clauses cue rising and falling pitch contours although readers might tend to break these clauses up when revoiced, resulting in additional pitch contours that do not correspond to formal clause boundaries. In phrasing such as "consciously looking for oddities because he had grasped the germ of the key insight," there is a variety of choices for what words to stress. If, from the context, *consciously* was considered new or important information, the reader might stress it, placing less emphasis on *looking;* he could accent *cause* in *because* to underscore the causal importance of why Morris might be so diligent about his search; or he could stress *oddities* to place more weight on the fact that it is just those oddities that constitute the most important finds. Grammar and punctuation provide some cues to interpretation but readers are also left to supply much on their own, based on their experience both with language and with the context, which in this case includes what the reader has already learned from the preceding pages of *Wonderful Life.*

Literary genres perhaps come closest to making use of the "voiced" properties that emanate from intonation, pausing, pitch, and so forth because literary writers have relatively more freedom in their use of language. Literary dialogue, for example, can consist of sentence fragments, one-word responses, italicized words and phrases, phonological spellings ("I dunno," "you don't forgit nuth'n") and is often framed by narrated indications as to how a word is said by a character (angrily, saucily, in a monotone, with a shudder). Literary features like alliteration and onomatopoeia intensify the voiced quality of the discourse, and literary dialogue likewise makes use of stylistic markers that provide specific cues for revoicing.

In the following example from *Emma*, ([1816] 1957) Jane Austen takes advantage of certain conventions of literary dialogue to help signal a particular revoicing tone. In the passage, Emma is responding to a comment by her friend and sometime antagonist, Mr. Knightley.

> This [comment] Emma felt was aimed at her; and it made her quite angry. It was not in compliment to Jane Fairfax however that he was so indifferent, or so indignant; he was not guided by *her* feelings in reprobating the ball, for *she* enjoyed the thought of it to an extraordinary degree. It made her animated—open hearted—she voluntarily said;—
>
>   "Oh! Miss Woodhouse, I hope nothing may happen to prevent the ball. What a disappointment it would be! I do look forward to it, I own, with *very* great pleasure." (199)

The first paragraph of the excerpt is a description of Emma's thoughts, what she "feels" or is thinking, rather than objective narrative. This, together with a sense that the reader may have that Emma is angry, cues a "voicing" of the passage that reflects her anger. To voice a strident, angry tone, a reader might elevate the pitch on the first syllable of *compliment* or *Fairfax* or *reprobating* more than if the contextual indication were for sadness.

There are thus a number of ways to revoice individual words. Here italics and exclamation marks cue emphasis; commas, dashes, and semicolons mark pauses; quotation marks signify a change in speaking voice. Repetition ("so indifferent, or so indignant") might serve to accentuate "so" when revoiced and indicate a particular interpretation. The selection, of course, depends on a range of factors that are determined only in part by cuing of a particular passage. Among these factors is the narrative context. Is the speaker being sarcastic, for example, or ironic, or naively ebullient? Should the word *Oh* be revoiced in a drawn-out glide, or quickly, staccato-like, or with rising or falling pitch contour? Should it be pronounced loudly or softly—that is, does the exclamation mark call for loudness or does it indicate surprise or curtness? How has Jane Fairfax, the speaker in the second paragraph, normally responded to Emma or to other characters in the preceding pages? Most important, however, is how a particular reader's personal linguistic history militates for certain characteristics in the revoicing. This history would include a reader's assessment of how someone "sounds" when angry as well as the reader's intonational style in talk to himself or his familiars. It would also be influenced by the reader's experience with *Emma*, the reading of the work in its entirety—not simply a short excerpt—and by the reader's familiarity with both nineteenth-century novels and literature as a whole. Finally, some choices are indeed linked to one's actual speaking voice—how one actually sounds when speaking, and thus, in this sense, revoicing is personal, a feature that speaks to the uses to which voice has most commonly been put in composing and textual analysis.

Visual Comprehension—Using Eyes *and* Ears

Despite the power of revoicing, it is quite likely that the visual processing of texts influences understanding far more than it is given credit for under theories that use voice as a controlling metaphor, whether it be in textual production, analysis, or processing. For reasons I have laid out earlier, we are culturally focused on the spoken word, so much so that we slight the extensive realm of the visual. Chafe's study (cited earlier), for example, neglected to consider that punctuation may not consistently require auditory imaging to do the job. In fact, writers often call upon rules of punctuation that have less to do with how a stretch of discourse sounds when read or spoken aloud than with more-or-less arbitrary conventions about, say, where a comma is supposed to go in noun strings. So that while what Chafe presents is very suggestive about our faculty of "giving voice" to a text in order to understand it, understanding may very well involve reconstructing texts in a way that not only accesses our revoicing capabilities but makes use of our knowledge about how texts should look. Understanding a written text, it would seem, is neither exclusively a visual phenomenon nor an aural one.

Other, more explicit examples abound. Italicized words stand out visually; they are different from the other words. Reading an italicized word would translate into emphasis, precluding the necessity to vocalize that word in order to comprehend stress. In other words, an italicized word need not cue loudness or pitch change in order to make sense and set that word apart from the rest of the nonitalicized text. Paragraphing can mark a topic shift visually and doesn't need a theory of revoicing to account for this. Other formatting options—facilitated by the computer age—such as word size, font selections, direction and orientation of print, all suggest that as texts change and readers become more sophisticated, revoicing has less of an influence and visual comprehension more in the processing of texts (see Chapter 7).

Competent readers skim quickly over written passages, skipping words and punctuation, so that revoicing, at best, might be an abbreviated activity. Speed-readers or readers engaged in skimming arguably employ both visual and aural reading. They pick out only words or word clusters to obtain an abbreviated message of what is on the page, and the quickness with which they work suggests a reliance on the relatively faster-working visual operations. It may also be that speed-readers revoice (and hear) fragments, and much as listeners do when overhearing fragments from a conversation in another room, speed-readers "fill in the blanks," reconstructing the missing parts to produce meaningful sentences. This operation is a very rapid one, so rapid that it is difficult to tease out precisely how the processing works. It may be that speed-readers don't use revoicing at all in skimming or speed-reading, that the activity is iconic reading, like the reading of numbers. This could account for speed-readers often having difficulty remembering passages read; their access to echoic memory and aural long-term memory is either shut off or circumvented. It should be noted, however, that speed-readers also spend less time with the text, and this is likely one important reason that they generally forget what they have read more quickly.

Readers working with texts of high surface difficulty (e.g., texts written in a complex style unfamiliar to them) read more slowly in order to understand; revoicing every word may become a necessity. A person who has minimal familiarity with physics, for example, may revoice much of a textbook on astrophysics. By contrast, texts of low surface difficulty (e.g., a contemporary novel) may require far less of the inner ear because readers can move through the texts more rapidly. For example, a mystery or detective novel—especially if a reader can make predictions not only about plotting but about the kind of language he will encounter (lexicon and syntax)—may be processed visually. Other types of novels may force readers to listen. Henry James works with a fairly familiar lexicon, but, stylistically, his prose is constructed in such a way that if the reader does not get the prosody right, the work (or sentence or paragraph, etc.) is incomprehensible. Especially in novels such as *The Golden Bowl* where a single sentence can last for several pages, James' text forces the reader to revoice, or, in Baddeley's terms, to make maximum use of the Articulatory Loop, in order to understand.

Some reading experts, notably Frank Smith, believe that reading is, in important part, a top-down activity, that is, readers make predictions about what they are reading and use the text to confirm or disconfirm those predictions. Smith argues that readers look at a word shape, predict what that word will be, and don't necessarily rely upon phonetics or phonology in decoding. Bottom-up reading is decoding individual letters and words and piecing them together in order to understand the whole; bottom-up reading utilizes phonological translation. He argues—and this is currently the prevailing wisdom—that good readers use both approaches, combining both data-driven and conceptually driven strategies, employing both phonological decoding, visual shape of words, and prediction to read.

Very compelling evidence for visual processing comes from studies of reading for the hearing-impaired. In *Language and Deafness* (1984), Stephen Quigley and Peter Paul argue that good readers who are hearing-impaired—assuming that these readers have or have had some access to an aural world—use both strategies, relying partly on visual processing and partly on phonological decoding. Hearing-impaired readers who are poor readers use a kind of visual gestalt to process texts; they exist in a world in which seeing must help compensate for what they cannot hear, and naturally, "seeing" is primary in their reading of texts. Gaines, Mandler, and Bryant (1981) speculate that their approach is exclusively top-down since they have no access to phonological storage.

In "Written Language in a Visual World" (1981), J. G. Kyle contends that the extreme difficulty that prelingually deaf children have in learning to read and write may have something to do with the difficulty in accessing their Articulatory Loop (see Baddeley, discussed previously). Whether or not the Articulatory Loop is a useful model for what actually happens in processing text, the fact that the prelingually deaf do not have the same direct access to the hearing of physical voices means they do not have "voiced" models; hence they must learn to read in ways that don't include the human speaking voice and, consequently, their writing may look (and sound in our nondeaf, revoiced language) much different.

But the limited access that the hearing-impaired have to an auditory environment also restricts their world knowledge as well, indicating that the inability to use the "inner voice" or the "inner ear" may not be what makes it more difficult to read. Because they are often totally shut off from the oral communication, many deaf readers come to the activity of reading without the same contextual knowledge as hearing persons; thus, predictions they do make about what they are reading may be inaccurate or misleading. One result is that hearing-impaired readers are often very skillful at understanding the overall message or gist of a text, but are very poor at grasping details.

Silences and Empty Spaces

In Chapter 1, I cited Seymour Chatman, who argued that voice is a presence that we sense by "reading between the lines." This implies that there is something nontextual that the reader supplies and then can identify as a presence. By contrast, Wolfgang Iser (1978), sees these nontextual areas as "gaps" that result because the reader has different goals, plans, and behaviors than the writer and the text the writer has produced. For Iser, it is within these gaps that the reader makes projections, drawing upon her world knowledge and experience to make sense out of what she reads. Real communication between text and reader— and this resonates with Bakhtin's notion of "understanding"—occurs when the text motivates changes in the reader's projections, and when the reader gives up some of her original projections to accommodate the text. According to Iser, a text stimulates the reader to use her store of knowledge to complete a text; as such, a text is indeterminate because the writer has little or no control over the reader's response, even though some cues and indications have been given by the text. Clearly, if the presence of a voice lies between the lines (or in the gaps), it is amorphous and undefined.

In written discourse, silences have a physical, spatial aspect. Spacing conventions, paragraphing, or chapter breaks cue changes in meaning, although a pause may or may not occur in the actual revoicing. Should the reader pause, as cued by the spacing between chapters of a book, for example, the text is silent. Alternately, he may move directly to the next chapter without a break, much like speakers in a conversation who make topic shifts without pausing. The chapter break is the physical marker that designates a new reading orientation, calling upon the reader's knowledge of chapter conventions and asking the reader to make the requisite shift.

Laurence Sterne's *Tristram Shandy* contains some unusual instances of utilizing blanks; the novel's Chapters 18 and 19 in Volume 9 are blank pages. The text is silent, or at least the *idea* of silence is invoked, but the text continues to convey meaning. That is, the blank chapters are meaningful; the reader fills in the blanks.

Poetry makes even more specialized use of the page in its line spacing and blocking of the text and individual words. But again the reading is not a monologic phenomenon. In order for these blanks to be interpreted as pauses or silences or spaces where there is no sound between blocks of text, they need to be *interpreted* as silences. Moreover, while it is conceivable that one can read over a block of text containing spaces, paragraph breaks, and chapter breaks without a pause, the revoicing invokes those pauses in a kind of mental shorthand that depends upon visual processing. The following is a poem I sketched out for the purpose of illustration. It is loosely crafted after the style of e.e. cummings:

       Three trees
              (willow)
      drugged
      tripping-   ing

o-
ver

untuned gustsofair

splaying leaves
            branches   twigs   detritus
                        and deafness

along the gutters of use

and finally

in
April, can anyone untangle

the seasons?

It is quite possible that in the revoicing of it—especially if it is read over rapidly or aloud for an audience—the poem may lose all or part of the effect of its spatial design. On the other hand, the spacing is important to the meaning and the impact of the poem, and this may manifest itself only in the visual conceptualization of the poem. The reader may understand the pauses iconically, processing the physical aspect of the blocking and incorporating that into his understanding. Hence, revoicing is not operative, and using voice as a metaphor for this kind of spatial understanding is to deny the importance of the sense of sight.

Lessons for Pedagogy

For a long time now I have been a proponent of reading aloud: teacher to student, student to student, writer to herself, reader to himself. Not only is this an effective pedagogical tool for poetry and fiction, but it serves a useful purpose for all kinds of writing from laboratory reports to expository essays. Reading aloud helps writers and readers tap into their aural imaging, and understand at a visceral level the rhythms, contours, and tones of written text. Although there is no direct evidence as to pedagogical benefit—partly because that kind of evidence would require being able to look through the brain with a flashlight and a roadmap and scientifically we are not quite there yet—the voicing research that I have introduced here suggests that an aural component is tied into reading and writing at important levels, especially in novice readers and writers.

But this is not the same as voice in any of the multiple connotations I have laid out previously in this book. Voice as a metaphor has to do with feeling-hearing-sensing a person behind the written words, even if that person is just a persona created for a particular text or a certain reading. The voice that I refer to in this chapter is the literal voice, and it may be valuable for the student to be aware and make use of. Most people who work in writing centers or writing labs or do any extensive work with students in one-on-one conferencing know, at least intuitively or anecdotally, the value of reading texts aloud. Whether the student reads the paper aloud or the teacher does, mistakes are often readily caught; awkward wording or phrasing is discovered; and a writer's awareness of an audience is heightened. In revoicing, the adding of intonation, stress, pitch, and other prosody, both writer and reader tap into their aural imaging—comparing and contrasting what is read aloud with patterns in their language competence. In a way, they are accessing the *langue*, their internal knowledge of language, but this kind of knowledge is sensory, having to do with sounds. It is not, however, more "internal" or closer to consciousness than other senses; it is simply one of the tools of stylistic awareness.

The second lesson is to pay renewed respect to the visual components of texts. The creation and expansion of business and technical writing instruction—where visual presentation is a crucial part of the rhetorical package—as well as the development of word processing sophistication among students and teachers both contribute to an increasing attention to the look of the page. I am not only speaking about formatting but about visual grammar as well. Visual grammar may include choices of punctuation, considerations about lexical size and shape of words, syntactical and spatial constructions such as simple and compound sentences—all of which may affect the reading, and none of which has to do with voicing alone.

Ultimately, what I am advocating here is not a new idea but a new approach. Teachers have often asked students to pay attention to form and to their audiences. Some teachers are more specific, urging students to attend not just to how they write but to how readers read, to what readers do or do not bring to the act of reading (as a result of their world knowledge) or to how they follow cuing devices such as transitions or logical connectors (that help in prediction). We don't very often see the pedagogical value to reading aloud to a first-year college writing class or a graduate technical writing class, nor do we often enough have students consider how readers might process an argument visually.

While these suggestions will hardly be the panaceas to resolve all writing problems, they might help some writers work more productively than if we ask them to search and find something as nebulous and difficult as a voice. In the next few chapters, I will continue my discussion of audience and visual literacy in the context of metaphors from different fields that may provide practical alternatives.

Notes

1. It should be noted that the concept of "natural" versus "stylized" is not uncontroversial. However, the discussion that would be required to do this concept justice would take us too far afield from the present argument.

2. See John J. Gumperz, *Discourse Strategies* (Cambridge: Cambridge UP, 1982), for a thorough discussion on the effects of contextualization cues on intonation. See also Deborah Tannen, *Talking Voices: Repetition, Dialogue, and Imagery in Conversational Discourse* (Cambridge: Cambridge UP, 1989).

Chapter Six

Voices from Women's Studies

In this chapter, I will look at alternatives to voice that come from feminism and women's studies. At the heart of this discussion is my conviction that voice is a pivotal metaphor for a tradition that has systematically privileged what is Western, what is white, and what is male, and that in using voice to articulate a struggle for the accretion of status and authority, marginalized groups, including women, are subscribing not only to the same language as the patriarchal system that they have struggled against but, as a necessary consequence, to the same value systems and ideology as well.

Although it may be obligatory for marginalized groups to be fluent in the language of the status quo in order to transform it, I don't believe that the use of voice does us any good at all; in fact it may constrain our thinking about power and language. As we have seen, voice is not only very pervasive; it is also widely considered to have enormous explanatory power by those who use it. Furthermore it is solidly attached to a political agenda. Interestingly, feminist and women's studies—which are also connected to political agendas—are extraordinarily rich metaphorically, with voice being only one of numerous metaphorical schema that figure within their discourses. I will examine some powerfully suggestive alternative metaphors and explore how they might be productive and meaningful alternatives to voice and its entailments, not only for women but for all of us.

The Language of the Feminists

Feminists are acutely aware of how language governs ways of being in the world. Nelly Furman writes:

It is through the medium of language that we define and categorize areas of difference and similarity, which in turn allow us to comprehend the world around us. Male-centered categorizations predominate in American English and subtly shape our understanding and perception of reality; this is why attention is increasingly directed to the inherently oppressive aspects for women of a male-constructed language system. (in Showalter 1985, 253)

Shoshana Felman speaks of the need to "reinvent" language,

> . . . to speak not only against, but outside of the specular phallogocentric structure, to establish a discourse the status of which would no longer be defined by the phallacy of masculine meaning. (in Showalter 1985, 254)

Still, many feminists find themselves at once repudiating the language of the status quo while being dependent upon it. When Annie Leclerc in *Parole de femme* articulates her perception of the goal of feminism, "to invent a language that is not oppressive, a language that does not leave speechless but that loosens the tongue" (in Showalter 1985, 253), her locution "loosens the tongue" implicitly values the one who talks (who has a voice), leaving us in the same metaphorical situation as we have been since Plato; those who talk are subjugators, and those who are silent are oppressed.

Arguments to seek a new language go hand-in-hand with arguments to promote new canonical texts to study, appreciate, and promote in our teaching of literary culture. In "A Literature of Their Own" (1985) Elaine Showalter argues for a new canon of women's literature, one that would provide a basis upon which to build a women's literary criticism. But Toril Moi (1985) is skeptical about this enterprise, arguing that Showalter is merely replicating humanist values. Moi maintains that the humanist,

> believes in literature as an excellent instrument of education: by reading 'great works,' the student will become a finer human being. The great author is great because he (occasionally even she) has managed to convey an authentic vision of life; and the role of the reader or critic is to listen respectfully to the voice of the author as it is expressed in the text. . . . But a new canon [as Showalter argues for] would not be intrinsically less oppressive than the old. The role of the feminist critic is still to sit quietly and listen to her mistress's voice as it expresses authentic female experience. The feminist reader is not granted leave to get up and challenge this female voice; the female text rules as despotically as the old male text. (78)

Not insignificantly, Moi's use of the voice metaphor illustrates its strong association with traditional humanist values; furthermore, the language we use is inevitably linked not only to how we read, write, and think, but to what we read, write, and think. In order to resist patriarchal language and values (or those of any dominant discourse), we need to look hard at the metaphors we unconsciously or consciously use and consider them in light of alternatives that might refocus our thinking on linguistic and epistemological possibilities. Before I propose alternatives, I want to look at liability and possibility in two recent and very well-known works that have been enormously influential in shaping how we think about women's rhetoric.

Searching (Listening) for the Woman's Voice

Carol Gilligan's *In a Different Voice* (1982) and Mary Field Belenky, Blythe McVicker Clinchy, Nancy Rule Goldberger, and Jill Mattuck Tarule's *Women's Ways of Knowing* (1986) are both concerned with the emergence of the female voice in a world traditionally monopolized by patriarchal discourse. Through their studies of conversations with women about their view of the world and themselves, Gilligan and Belenky et al. provide compelling insights into the maturation and structure of feminine consciousness.

Gilligan

Carol Gilligan's "Letter to Readers," which introduces the 1993 edition of her book *In a Different Voice* (note that the "Letter" also appears in Peter Elbow's *Landmark Essays on Voice and Writing* [1994]), immediately starts out with a discussion on the importance of voice. Early on, she refers to the influence of Kristin Linklater, a voice teacher in the theater, on her own recent work.

> Linklater speaks of 'freeing the natural voice' . . . and what she means is that you can hear the difference between a voice that is an open channel—connected physically with breath and sound, psychologically with feelings and thoughts, and culturally with a rich resource of language—and a voice that is impeded or blocked. (xv)

But while Gilligan introduces her discussion of women's voice with this reference to the literal speaking voice, she is not simply referring to spoken language. In linking psychology, culture, and naturalness with voice, she delves into epistemology, into ways of perceiving the world and into ways of knowing and understanding the self. So while Gilligan says, "By voice, I mean voice" (xvi), she apparently means much more. First, she means a kind of communicative energy that emanates from deep inside a person, from the heart of a person's being. Voice, she explains, "is something like what people mean when they speak of the core of the self." And voice is "a powerful psychological instrument and channel, connecting inner and outer worlds" (xvi). Within this inner world, which as a core is ostensibly stable, there is a personal (and perhaps universal) truth or set of truths. And these are what women need to be able to tap into and bring out into the world, connecting what is going on in their inner lives with what they experience in their environments.

Significantly, Gilligan links this inner self with spoken language, or, at least, the oral tradition:

> At present, I find that women writers, and especially African-American poets and novelists who draw on an oral/aural tradition and also on searing and complex experiences of difference, are taking the lead in voicing an art that responds to the question which now preoccupies many people: how to give voice to difference in a way that recasts our discussion of relationship and the telling of truth. (xvii)

But while Gilligan assumes that women may function within an epistemology that is distinct from men, and while their voices must be different in order to "be themselves" and articulate that difference, the linguistic (metaphorical) apparatus through which these differences are perceived and communicated is painfully similar to the patriarchal epistemological structures that have characterized Western civilization to this day. In particular, the emphasis on the existence of a stable inner truth echoes the kind of Platonic logocentrism that deconstructionists and postmodernists have worked so hard to dislocate (see Chapter 2). Furthermore, in connecting oral traditions with truth-telling under the rubric of voice, Gilligan also participates in the kind of phonocentrism that has traditionally, in Western civilization, honored speech (over writing) as closest to one's innermost thoughts. Thus the language Gilligan uses here to articulate her position is precisely the language that Moi, Felman, and other feminists are so critical of.

But while the values implicit in Gilligan's discussion have unfortunate resonance with those values that are so prominent in patriarchal discourse, it would be inaccurate to say that her conception of voice merely replicates those values in the same ways. In fact, Gilligan goes to some lengths to update the concept, tying voice to culture, context, and social construction, precisely to emphasize the *relational* aspect of voice that is so significant to the women that Gilligan studied: "To have something to say is to be a person. But speaking depends on listening and being heard; it is an intensely relational act" (xvi). Gilligan continues:

> Relationship requires connection. It depends not only on the capacity for empathy or the abilities to listen to others and learn with language or take their point of view, but also on having a voice and having a language. The differences between women and men which I describe

center on a tendency for women and men to make different relational errors—for men to think that if they know themselves, following Socrates' dictum, they will also know women, and for women to think that if only they know others, they will come to know themselves. (xviii)

These different "relational errors" are germane to the concept of voice that emerged in the 1960s, wherein student writers were encouraged to "put themselves" into their writing to make it have resonance—resonance with the reader—and to place an identifiable stamp on how they expressed what they believed. To accomplish this, it would seem that the writers would either have to know themselves first or find themselves in their early drafts. If, however, the writer uses her reading and writing to know others, or even to situate herself among others, it becomes difficult, if not impossible, to put oneself in one's writing first and foremost; the purpose of the kind of writing promulgated by voice proponents of the 1960s and 1970s is not to know others; it is to be heard by others and even to extend power over others. As I pointed out in an earlier chapter, it's difficult to imagine even what *voice*—in the sense of establishing yourself or a self into the writing or the writing context—might mean. Stylistically, for example, what kinds of linguistic features bear the stamp of a self? How does the vocabulary or syntax of a stretch of written discourse convey a unique, living, breathing person? To approach this issue from another direction, does a woman who writes to explore relationships write without resonance? Or will her writing necessarily fail to engage an audience because it doesn't necessarily champion a voice but rather seeks to forge a relationship between a reader and writer in which the writer is not necessarily the source of control?

Voice proponents would argue that voices exist within this transaction, that the writer needs an authoritative tone to open up reader/writer relationships. But even if one considers voice in its multidimensional, relational sense, the ramifications and entailments of the voice metaphor are essentially the same, however it is applied, and this is the central problem with using voice at all; it is inherently masculinist. Women who seek to have a voice seem to be searching for "a different voice," which one might presume is still powerful, distinctive, and resonant—even though it is "theirs." Because Elbow and Gilligan are interested in how discourse resonates between speaker and listener, writer and reader, it seems that the goals are, if not the same, at least strikingly similar.

Nonetheless, a review of Gilligan's work reveals that there is more at work in women's struggles than the acquisition of a distinctive voice. Gilligan talks about the conflicts many women have in distinguishing between what they feel comfortable saying, doing, and being and what they are required to say, do, and be within their environment. Gilligan insists that "they *can* hear the difference" between what they want to say and what they're supposed to say. But the problem seems to be that "being themselves" doesn't afford women power in a world where strong, male voices are loudest and most dominant because they are already in positions of control. Even after decades of social turmoil, men still do most of the judging and rewarding in important aspects of life: government, business, family. For women, then, is making their voices heard actually where the gratification and satisfaction—or even their power—lies? It would seem preferable to many of the women in Gilligan's study to have their *ways of being* in the world, however these ways become manifest, legitimized by themselves and others. And because language is crucial to the expression and promotion of those ways of being, women's god terms—the key terms that influence and activate all other terms—should not necessarily be those cherished by the status quo. In other words, if shouting (or speaking loud and long, or dominating the conversation) confers power, and women want some of that power, do they simply need to add to the noise? According to Gilligan's study and many others (including Belenky et al., that I will discuss next), women aren't generally as interested in dominating the floor. In fact, one could argue that women have other significant and very powerful ways of being in the world that go beyond voice; I will explore these rich possibilities in the pages to come.

Women's Ways of Knowing and the Web

Belenky, Clinchy, Goldberger, and Tarule also make use of the voice metaphor. In the introduction, they explain that women they interviewed were often inclined to describe their experiences in terms of voice as if "the development of a sense of voice, mind, and self were intertwined" (18) or as if by having a stronger, more unified voice, they could achieve the kind of self-respect and respect from others that has traditionally been conferred on men.

One of the central problems that Belenky et al. tackle—and justifiably so—is the scenario that seems to be perpetuated everywhere, in families, at work, in school: where men are speakers and women are listeners.

> The continued injunction against articulating needs, feelings, and experiences must constrain the development of hearts and minds, because it is through speaking and listening that we develop our capacities to talk and to think things through. The fact that women are

expected to curtail their voice may account for the greater prevalence
of clinical depression and learned helplessness among women than
among men. (167)

If men are the speakers and men have greater social control over
their lives and the lives of others, then it appears to make sense that
women who seek to garner some of that control would also aspire to be
speakers.

Belenky et al. compare the aural metaphor of voicing to visual metaphors that often appear in the language of logic used by scientists and
philosophers. One example is the use of light, as in *illuminate, enlighten,*
or *see,* which implies objectifying distance as well as clarification. These
visual metaphors presumably help convey the impression of objectivity
that physical or spatial distance affords. Belenky et al. argue that speaking and listening require proximity, and that given many of the metaphors the women in their study used to describe their lives ("speaking
out," "being silenced," "words as weapons," "saying what you mean"),
this proximity seems more important to women than to men (18).

But whether or not voice is helpful in enabling women to be proudly
and powerfully themselves in a patriarchal society is open to question.
In their opening chapter, Belenky et al. talk about one of the subjects
of their study, "Ann," as "locked in a world of silence" (23). She had
trouble talking in school because she felt dumb. She says, "If I tried to
explain something and someone told me that it was wrong, I'd burst
into tears over it" (23). Belenky et al. refer to this as the absence of
voice, a concept that is not unlike Elbow's notion of "voiceless prose."
Both uses imply a lack of confidence and authority and are linked to
how fully the speaker perceives herself to have captured the attention
of the reader/listener. But it is not that Ann or the writers of voiceless prose don't have voices. Ann certainly has a voice, even though
she considers it faltering or stymied; and if any writing has voice, it all
does. These just may be the wrong voices because they lack authority.
Thus, having a voice does not axiomatically confer power or instill self-
confidence. These women, who Belenky et al. say are the youngest
and "most socially, economically and educationally deprived" (23–24),
simply have not had the same kinds of opportunities to learn the dominant (and, we would have to say, patriarchal) discourse as women of a
different social status; that is, they haven't been able to acquire a voice
that would be acceptable in the language community in which they operate—the same community that holds power over their lives. Simi-
larly, student texts written in pseudo-erudite academic or legalistic
prose aren't necessarily silent or voiceless. Rather, the readers, teachers, analysts don't recognize those voices because they don't conform to
the "sounds" of authenticity or authority that the readers have come to
associate with traditional rhetorical power. Consequently these writers

and these women are excluded and made to doubt themselves. If we subscribe to the theory that one's sense of self is derived from these social interactions, this exclusion could be tantamount to having the self reduced to nothing.

Silence, of course, can be a source of enormous power when it is used by choice rather than as the only alternative. In fact, in a postmodern world in which truth is considered unstable, where contexts and participants are volatile and changeable, where control of any rhetorical circumstance is momentary or illusory, silence may be the only authentic response. In fact, while women in *Women's Ways of Knowing* are not at ease with their own silence, they do seem to be able to embrace the volatility that characterizes life without apparently wanting to tame it, and they seem to be quite comfortable with ambiguity. These women may want control over their lives, but they don't necessarily want to belong to the dominant communities of utterly secure and consequently static, confident, and voiced selves. A woman in the study comments:

> I'm a different person each day. It's the day, I guess, depending on how it is outside or how my body feels. (83)

And another woman:

> I only am the person that I am at this moment. Tomorrow I'm somebody different, and the day after that I'm somebody different. . . . I'm always changing. Everything is always changing. (83)

The women perceive both themselves and their world as in flux, and many of the women in these studies seem very predisposed to accepting this inherent instability.

One of most interesting metaphors that emerges from this book focuses attention on the interdependency of communities and families and on the work that Carol Gilligan has done to demonstrate and celebrate this interdependency. Belenky et al. recommend that the "guiding" metaphor for this interdependency is the *web*. This metaphor—which not insignificantly figures large in the metaphorical schema of computer technology (see Chapter 7)—

> suggest[s] a complexity of relationships and the delicate interrelatedness of all so that tension and movement in one part of the system will grow to be felt in all parts of the whole. In the complexity of a web, no one position dominates over the rest. Each person—no matter how small—has some potential for power; each is always subject to the actions of others. (178)

Belenky et al. contrast this metaphor with the concept of the autonomous self who must relate to others via bonds of agreement in a kind of pyramid structure, where indeed one person holds sway over others.

At this point, I want to consider the web in more detail. The web is connotatively rich with definitions stemming from its reference to the web that a spider weaves to the connective tissue within the body. The spider's web is a gossamer-like structure composed of sticky, delicate strands designed to ensnare or entangle the spider's prey. With this association we might understand how the sense of power (the spider's, the web's itself) over an environment depends upon how well the web is constructed, where it is located, and any number of other environmental factors including weather, human or animal interference, even acts of God. Its success as a web depends on its relationships and how it handles them. At the same time, the spider's web is a highly fragile thing, tenuous in its weave, easily broken yet easily repaired and quite complex. Interestingly, although there is infinite variety in the weave of a web, its size and shape are constrained by its function, site, and creator (the spider).

Applying discourse to this particular connotation of web has some interesting results. The web of discourse is potentially ensnaring or entrapping, particularly in a rhetorically effective argument or piece of poetry or prose fiction. When this is the goal of the author, we could call ensnaring discourse to be highly effective. Often our metaphors reflect this, as in "I was really caught up in this discussion" or "I can't put this book down" or "Her reasoning really had me." Interestingly, this connotation has some synchronicity with the kind of rhetorical manipulation that Plato associated with writing and rhetoric (see Chapter 1) where, in the wrong hands, it has power to corrupt an unwitting audience.

But it also highlights the interconnectedness: the working together of parts, the influence of contexts, and the link between creator, environment, and materials. The strength is in the connectedness or weave. Note that entomologically, *text* comes from the Medieval Latin word *textus* meaning "texture" or "context" and from the past participle of the Latin *texere*, which means "to weave." The implications for written text are numerous. Texts are woven together, and the result is a particular texture, enmeshed within a specific and often unique context. Writers may initiate the weaving, but they must work with others and with contexts.

One of the consequences of considering texts in terms of texture and webs is that we can redefine attention to craft, style, and form, which tends to be overlooked in a voice pedagogy in the interest of avoiding the stylistic formalism that typified the kinds of academic (and student) essays that troubled Macrorie, Elbow, and others. For voice proponents, the emphasis on tapping into the authorial presence and communicating that presence to a reader was a way of making student writing more interesting and dynamic. Even when we acknowledge that writers have many voices, the focus for voicists is less on textuality, craft, and style than it is on a kind of energy, often mysteriously accessed, that somehow gets transferred from writer to reader through the actions of a text. Attention to craft in a paper that is being considered as a web or a texture might ask the writer (or reader) to consider connections and disconnections (of a web) or intricacy or simplicity (of the weave), all of which the reader is an integral part. For example, transition words or logical connectors may help connect or weave together disparate parts for a reader. Emotive language may tie a particular theme to concerns the reader might have. Craft, among other things then, might involve attention to the links and junctions. This kind of conceptualization has the potential of being more explicit and hence more practical to teach than voice, and hence can produce more tangible results in improving one's writing style.

There are other particulars about a web that show promise both for textual analysis and pedagogy. First, the web is a very appropriate metaphor for the kind of literary analysis I worked with in Chapter 1 on Atwood's *Bodily Harm*. In exploring the web, the weave, or the textures of language in the novel, the critical spotlight is not just on the complexity of literary language and structure but on the way features, both lexical and syntactic, work together aggregatively, each new element or feature compounding the meaning of what has already been written/read. The web is a way of understanding how meaning proliferates rather than remains static.

For pedagogy, the web highlights interconnectedness not only of one word or phrase to the next in students' text but of their texts to the readers' "texts" or to texts already written or those that are to come. Students can work on the weave of their work, and can readily perceive that, much like a spider's web, their words can be rewoven or respun and the web reshaped to repair faulty communications or to accomplish different ends. Thus, the strength and effectiveness of a web is not uniquely in the *presence* of a voice, but in the sticky interconnections.

Voice, evolving as it has from its 1970s affiliations with powerful writing, carries with it connotations of an authentic and unitary self that prevent it from fitting very neatly into the web structure. First, the web is a spatial metaphor while voice is aural. Webs shift the emphasis, involving more than the voice in the interactions and interdependencies of discourse—human beings are, after all, more than voices; we are bodies taking up space, capable of movement at a variety of levels: physical, emotional, philosophical, and psychic. Silences, gestures, movements, and links to our environment—to contexts and participants—have more potential for signification when we consider rhetoric in terms of a web rather than of voices; these levels all signify. One could surely argue that webs can have voices, but within the metaphorical schema of the web, the emphasis is no longer focused on the producer of that voice or how that voice sounds; rather the weight is on the shifting affiliations and associations that the web makes metaphorically more explicit.

Unfortunately for web or network proponents, Belenky et al. still seem to hold dear the notion of authentic voice. This is a voice that allows people to "express themselves" fully and commands others to listen and respect what they have to say. Learning how to use one's authentic and "unique" voice, Belenky et al. argue, requires that a person "'jump outside' the frames and systems authorities provide and create their own frame" (134). But the creation of another frame may only provide a different way to hierarchize, potentially replicating the voice schema in which he who speaks loudest and longest dominates. There doesn't seem to be much that is new here, except for an equitable sharing of control, which, by the current statistics on women in power in government and business, has not come to pass.

Another problem with authentic voice is the concept of authenticity. What makes a voice authentic? We can watch a film at a movie theater, one that moves us very much, that resonates, that seems to convey authentic emotions, yet the author of the movie is a community of writers, producers, directors, actors, crew members, and audiences. One could argue, for example, that *Out of Africa* conveys a singular feel or presence that might characterize the stamp of an author. But whose voice is it? Isak Dineson, who wrote the short stories upon which it is based? Kurt Leudtke, who wrote the screenplay? Sydney Pollack, who directed the film? Meryl Streep or Robert Redford, who gave their interpretations to the words? Or the editors, camera crew, or climatic or geographical conditions on the set? Perhaps there is a "voice" we "hear" when a woman is truly free to say what she believes (whatever this means) or when a movie "speaks" to us, but the notion of authentic and unique voice masks the multileveled, chaotic, and dynamic paths and intersections that the web emphasizes.

Other Metaphorical Alternatives

Even if I have been successful at arguing that the web is a viable alternative to voice, it is not the only possibility. Many of the other alternatives that I suggest in the following sections are from feminist (loosely defined) writing and women's studies. The examples are intended to be suggestive; the categories are neither comprehensive nor discrete.

Fluid

In "This Sex Which Is Not One" (1985), Luce Irigaray makes the analogy between masculine/feminine and solid/liquid. Feminine discourse, she argues, is

> continuous, compressible, dilatable, viscous, conductible, diffusable. . . . That it is unending, powerful and impotent owing to its resistance to the countable; that it enjoys and suffers from a greater sensitivity to pressure; that it changes—in volume or in force, for example—according to the degree of heat; that is, in its physical reality, determined by friction between two infinitely neighboring forces—a dynamics of proximity and not the proper. (111)

What are the ramifications of fluid as a metaphor for discursive acts? First, fluids are less objectifiable than the male phallus, which is locatable and fixed, and hence ownable. As such, fluid enables us to understand how a speaker or writer can move easily from one subjectivity to another or blend subjectivities. In Chapter 4, I looked at how Frederic Jameson incorporates quotations from Althusser to make a point, and how this could be viewed as "managed discourse." A voicist critique might argue that Jameson's voice subjugates the voices of Althusser to do his bidding in the formulation of his argument, and that the Jameson subjectivity or voice and Althusser subjectivity or voice are in potential or real conflict, depending upon the skill of the author. Using *fluid,* we might avoid looking at written discourse as a battleground upon which voices fight to be heard but rather as a site in which multiple subjectivities are merged or interact. There are no winners or losers, no conquerors or defeated, not even any negotiated terrain (because negotiation brings with it a strong militaristic connotation of arbitration where there are still things lost and things won), but rather a coalescence of meanings and ideas. Note how a "fluid" discourse is one that flows well, is cohesive and connected, and is already valued in our lexicon about discourse and, in particular, writing.

In "The Laugh of the Medusa," Hélène Cixous (1980) is more specific about the fluid metaphor, connecting women's discourse to the sea:

> [W]e are ourselves sea, sand, coral, sea-weed, beaches, tides, swimmers, children, waves. . . . Heterogeneous, yes. For her joyous benefits she is erogenous; she is the erotogeneity of the heterogeneous: airborne swimmer, in flight, she does not cling to herself; she is dispersible, prodigious, stunning, desirous and capable of others, of the other woman that she will be, of the other woman she isn't, of him, of you. (260)

The specific character of the sea complicates fluid by adding the concepts of motion brought about by tides and geographic disruptions like land, earthquakes, and volcanoes and of contexts that provide fertile, nurturing environments for animals and plants. Fluid is visible, tactile, sensible, and sometimes audible, again opening up conceptions of discourse to sensory realms other than the aural. Further, it is "dispersible." It can exist as droplets or be absorbed into other elements, and this is a valuable attribute. If *voice* were dispersed, on the other hand, it would cease to be a voice or even recognizable sounds, losing its power. Integrity is important to voice, not to fluids.

The fluid metaphor does not exempt us from some of the problems we grapple with as writers and speakers. Discourse can be conceived in terms of floods (a surfeit of language), torrents (difficult to navigate), and trickles (too little substance). Perhaps the most controversial issue stems from the way the fluid metaphor forces us to redefine discursive boundaries. Intellectual property issues are deemphasized if discourse is fluid because there is no way to assess who contributed what; in fact boundaries become irrelevant, and, in Western culture, this is not an easy issue to dispense with. (See Chapter 4 for more discussion on this issue.)

Bodily Metaphors

Voice comes from the body. But for many feminist theorists, the body has a much more multifaceted role as a signifier than voice alone. Luce Irigaray, for example, compares the unitary quality of the male sex with the multiple female sex—consisting of lips, vagina, clitoris, cervix, uterus, breasts. A women's pleasure, she argues, is not single in form or unified, but rather multifold, multiform, and infinite.

Much like fluid, bodily metaphors help us move a conception of discourse beyond the aural (as in voice) and the visual (as in the observing, objective eye). One of the key senses that feminists underscore is the sense of touch; women, for example, can touch themselves and receive pleasure without anyone seeing. Fluid also invites connections to the sense of touch as in Luce Irigaray's notion of woman's style:

> This "style" does not privilege sight; instead, it takes each figure back to its source, which is among other things *tactile*. It comes back in touch with itself in that origin without ever constituting in it, constituting itself in it, as some sort of unity. *Simultaneity* is its "proper" aspect—a proper(ty) that is never fixed in the possible identity-to-self of some form or other. It is always *fluid*, without neglecting the characteristics of fluids that are difficult to idealize: those rubbings between two infinitely near neighbors that create a dynamics. Its "style" resists and explodes every firmly established form, figure, idea or con-

cept. Which does not mean that it lacks style, as we might be led to believe by a discursivity that cannot conceive of it. But its "style" cannot be upheld as a thesis, cannot be the object of a position. (79)

Interestingly, this conception of style stemming from the body defies the common metaphor that associates the body with a container. For example, Lakoff and Johnson (1980) argue that we perceive a whole range of worldly phenomenon in terms of containment.

> We are physical beings, bounded and set off from the rest of the world by the surface of our skins, and we experience the rest of the world as outside us. Each of us is a container, with a bounding surface and an in-out orientation. We project our own in-out orientation onto other physical objects that are bounded by surfaces. . . . But even when there is no natural physical boundary that can be viewed as defining a container, we impose boundaries—marking off territory so that it has an inside and a bounding surface. (29)

Containment makes unification feasible by virtue of the enclosed space. There are certainly other means to unify something, and there are certainly things within enclosed spaces that are not unified, but in setting limits, a writer—for example—has a finite set of particulars to deal with and organization is simply a process of moving them around. Boundaries enable control, and control means that elements within the container, while they have the capability for movement, don't have easy access to what is outside the container, that is, in the social world. Texts as containers become fairly static. (For more discussion, see Bowden 1993.)

Clearly, this way of understanding texts is only one approach. Irigaray and others are very aware of the sexual nature of the body and in particular a women's body and sexual being, and they champion this to counter the forces of containment. From Cixous:

> She [woman] lets the other language speak—the language of 1,000 tongues which knows neither enclosure nor death. To life she refuses nothing. Her language does not contain, it carries; it does not hold back, it makes possible. . . . I am spacious, singing flesh, on which is grafted no one knows which I, more or less human, but alive because of transformation. (260)

Without "enclosure" or containment, a sense of stability is in jeopardy. But this lack of stability also affords the perception of the body in, of, and with the world, interacting within social and natural realms.

The result for literary criticism and for composition pedagogy, of course, is far more equivocal and indeterminate than most people feel comfortable with—especially teachers and students who have been schooled into subscribing to the kind of stable, contained or self-contained, and unambiguous symbol-to-meaning correspondence that is prevalent in the traditional treatment of texts. Transformation, fluidity, multiplicity, and the multisensory are difficult to pin down. This is part of the reason that voice doesn't work very well. For voice to function in the ways it has been used to refer to writing, it needs enough integrity, specificity, and coherence for a reader to be able to identify it and to recognize when it doesn't "sound" right or changes; the reader can then study, even criticize, the text on that basis. For Irigaray and Cixous, *transformation* does not mean changing from one voice into another voice or voices—even though voice can and has been characterized as having some fluidity and adaptability. It means changing into other shapes or forms or even disintegrating. I suspect the concept of "morphing"—which is so popular in science fiction films where shapes "morph" into other shapes, some of them of this world and others not—may begin to approach the kind of transformation of a discursive entity in a text that these theorists are alluding to—precisely because it is an "entity" only temporarily, and usually changes enough in films so that the viewer comes to depend only upon the impermanent quality of the visible shape. In other words, the shapes are not dependable.

The Embrace

There is a bodily metaphor used in passing by Hélène Cixous that is particularly promising as an alternative to voice. In "The Laugh of the Medusa," Cixous distinguishes between a masculine domain and a feminine, marked by the "Realm of the Proper" and the "Realm of the Gift." The Proper, she argues, with its connections to property and appropriateness, is based on the promotion of self and dominance over others. The Gift, by contrast, is a property of woman.

> [I]t is paradoxically her capacity to depropriate unselfishly, body without end, without appendage, without principal "parts." . . . This doesn't mean that she's an undifferentiated magma, but that she doesn't lord it over her body or her desire. . . . Her libido is cosmic, just as her unconscious is worldwide. Her writing can only keep going, without ever inscribing or discerning contours, daring to make these vertiginous crossings of the other(s) ephemeral and passionate sojourns in him, her, them, whom she inhabits long enough to look at from the point closest to their unconscious from the moment they awaken, to love them at the point closest to their drive; and then further, impregnated through and through with these brief, identificatory embraces, she goes and passes into infinity. (259–260)

The embrace, as one might expect, has multiple meanings for the woman. First, embrace is what a woman's womb does to a penis (in the sexual act) or a child (in pregnancy); it is sexual act, reproductive act, and childbearing act, and these actions—and they are all actions not states—interconnect and interanimate. And, as we have seen in the studies by Gilligan and Belenky et al., the embrace also represents nicely how women in society respond to the world around them as well as how they order and organize experience.

In discourse, particularly in the writing classroom where voice still holds sway, voice tends to be used to focus attention on its producer (the writer), and then on which authorial voice the reader "hears." By contrast, embrace would focus more attention on the nature of the connection between writer and reader, facilitating a consideration of the effect of the text on an "embraced" audience.

The etymology is useful to consider. *Embrace* is from the Old French *embracier* or *en-* + *brace* (two arms), calling up the kinds of actions that take place when a person encircles some one or some thing within her arms: holding, loving by holding, caring, protecting, comforting but also holding someone against his will or forcibly moving him (and hence, manipulating). As such, embrace is a metaphor of power, both positive and negative—and occasionally both at the same time. It is a metaphor in which power struggles that involve holding and manipulation can potentially become explicit and can consequently be readily discussed and explored, particularly in terms of those kinds of ethical problems that have to do with the misuse or abuse of rhetorical power.

In other words, embrace can encourage more attention to the features about discourse that are not so apparent with voice. Voice proponents, at least initially in the 1970s and certainly in the ways voice is used today, see "writing with voice" in very positive, if not glowing, terms. It is only voice critics (See, for example, Hashimoto 1987, Leggo 1991) who, in their concern about the evangelical nature of voicists, worry about how voice may obfuscate or gloss over the negative effects of language hegemony. In other words, the classroom where students all have a right to their voice may not be as democratic or egalitarian or liberating as it is presumed to be. In a classroom filled with voices, literal or figurative, some voices will always be stronger, louder, and more powerful than others—especially if the goal is to find and use one's voice in writing. Attention to voice invites self-absorption, not just in the invention (e.g., freewriting) stage, but throughout the rhetorical activity. Moreover, when one person's voice takes over another's, the metaphor becomes more difficult to sustain (how does one voice taking over another voice "sound"?), except by deferring to the ventriloquism metaphor, and ventriloquism can mask the conflict of wills (although the idea of a master ventriloquist manipulating a puppet can and has been used to portray power inequities). It is not necessarily impossible to understand the manipulative aspect of discourse or rhetoric in using voice; rather embrace makes the maneuvering more clear. When a person embraces another, issues of control can be very explicit. An embrace can hold someone against his will, just as a reader of a powerful persuasive essay can be held against her will, unable to move freely, held captive (an entailment of embrace) to the language of the argument. Embrace can literally and figuratively move someone; in so doing, it coerces or wields power in ways that voice does not. While those who hear a voice can either respond or not listen, the embraced can hug back or resist, characterizing the interaction in different terms.

Embrace also invites some ways to talk about style. Just as one person can hold (or embrace) someone else with varying degrees of force, so an essay can "hold" an audience in analogous ways. Interestingly, the way someone is held cannot be isolated from the goal of the writer and the circumstances of the embrace. The writer may coerce a reader with emotional appeals or tease a reader with a provocative introduction; an embrace schema invites us to consider the maneuvering as well as understand the ways in which the audience (or persons embraced) responds, reacts, and resists or shapes the embrace. Embrace can be one of reciprocal passion. For example, a reader with strong opinions about the use of landmines—who perhaps even knows someone who has been maimed or killed by one—will respond strongly (passionately, emotionally) when encountering an argument to ban them. An embrace is often related to physicality including violent gestures or tender caresses, and thus can extend to fingers, directing attention to the sense of touch (tickle, tap, knock) and a consideration of touched surfaces (rough, smooth, wet, dry, soft, hard). The rhetorical analog is an almost visceral response to a text: raising blood pressure, producing goose bumps, or turning red in the face. The embrace works through proximity and can be potentially charged with feelings and emotions. The relationship between the embracer and the embraced is featured and complicated by thoughts, ideas, feelings, emotions, physicality, sexuality, and power.

With embrace there is difference and awareness of difference as well as the obfuscation of difference, for sometimes it's difficult to tell not only who is embracing, but where one person ends and the other begins, almost as if two people coalesce. In other words, the selves are not necessarily undifferentiated, and certainly they seem like discrete organisms when apart—that is, when not engaged in discourse—but those boundaries can become both less relevant and more complicated in an embrace. Interestingly, the locution "lost in an embrace" has a negative connotation and corresponds to concerns by proponents of voice preoccupied with the problem of having no voice or "losing one's voice" in their writing. If the purpose of an embrace is the coming together or the touching, "lost" is no longer as appropriate an adjective to describe the engagement of personae. In fact, the success of the embrace may at times be contingent upon how strongly the two personae connect or, even, intermingle, and how each is changed when they move apart.

An example from the composition classroom may be useful here to illustrate ways of using the embrace. In what has become a fairly common assignment in writing courses, a student is assigned to write a position paper, taking a stand on a controversial topic. Let's say that the topic is the legalization of illicit drugs. A situation in which the student is encouraged to use a strong voice for the assignment might entail that the student probe deeply into her own opinions on the subject and express them forcefully and clearly in the paper. She may be encouraged, of course, to use "a voice that is appropriate," which probably means she doesn't want to be too informal in her style. But the audience, even if stipulated in the assignment as "your peers" or "a general audience" usually remains quite abstract in the academic setting, leaving the student to grapple primarily with her position on the subject, the subject matter itself, and as shrewd an analysis as possible of what the teacher wants. Her focus includes her audience, but the idea of engaging an audience remains unfortunately hypothetical.

If, by contrast, the student were encouraged to conceptualize her writing as an embrace, she would be necessarily forced to consider—as would her teacher in designing the assignment and helping her complete it—ways in which she could *engage* her audience, grappling with style considerations (how to entice a reader into the embrace, how strongly to hold, how sensitively to touch, etc.) that would enable her to *hold* the embrace, and then leave her reader with the sensation of having *encountered* something significant.

The Dance

Another metaphor that emerges both from the bodily metaphors of women's studies—of which embrace is championed here—and from the literature by women on discursive practices is the dance. Although it is not a pivotal metaphor, many feminists have used it. Annette Kolodny, for example, entitles one of her essays "Dancing Through the Minefield," and the dance seems to represent both the patterned experiences of discourse and the precariousness of engaging in that discourse.

Louise Phelps (1988) refers to the "dance of discourse" in her *Composition as a Human Science,* not as a metaphor emerging from feminist studies but from modern conceptions of quantum physics (see 131–159). The "New Physics" deals with reality not as objects or particles but as events in flux (or in a dance) in which the observers and actors in these events are themselves part of the event. The interaction (or dance) is the focus.

The dance has considerable affinity with the bodily metaphors described here, and the fact that it has reverberations in other fields only adds to its explanatory power. The dance involves a kind of embrace with many of the attributes relating to style and function described here for the embrace. It differs in that it is, literally, a process with rhythmic patterns set to music. These patterns change according to participants, musical scores, and contexts, not unlike rhetoric, and these are infinitely variable. Good dancers, like good writers, can make the variations look effortless; novice dancers often appear clumsy even when they are sticking to a prescribed and repetitive pattern.

Although dances are given names (the fox trot, the samba, the twist), they usually are not dances unless they are actions or, better, interactions. They involve energy, and it is the charting of this energy that preoccupies both the new physicists and the new rhetoricians.

Conclusion

Many feminists would argue that the feminine "I" is quite different from the bold masculine "I" that is concerned with announcing his difference. Thus, when women use "voice" to describe powerful womanspeak or a woman's style, they mean something different from what men mean. For feminists in particular, any discussion of voice also casts it as diffused, displaced, or deferred, echoing some of the god terms of postmodernism. Perhaps the issue is the nature of rhetorical control. Moi points out, in criticizing Sandra Gilbert and Susan Gubar's *Madwoman in the Attic*, "The Phallus is often conceived of as a whole, unitary and simple form, as opposed to the terrifying chaos of the female genitals" (67). Chaos, of course, is threatening in a patriarchal society where control is the desired end product. If, however, chaos is viewed as a positive term—even if control is understood as a necessary counterbalance to chaos—the repercussions for pedagogy may be such that currently marginalized students (women, ethnic groups, ESL students) might find more accurate reflections of their worldview, which, quite often, celebrates plurality, movement, and disruption of traditional definitions and boundaries.

As I have pointed out in previous chapters in discussions of presence, authenticity, and individuality, the problem with voice is as much about the baggage it carries with it as it is its lack of efficacy in referring to things texts do. Perhaps it is a truism that we are continuously and irrevocably constrained to the past—both through our institutions, epistemology, and language. In her 1985 survey of Anglo-American feminists (Showalter, Kolodny, and Jehlen), Moi comments on the inevitability of this fact, even for the most radical feminists.

> [A]ll forms of radical thought inevitably remain mortgaged to the very historical categories they seek to transcend. But our understanding of this historically necessary paradox should not lead us complacently to perpetuate patriarchal practices. (88)

And perhaps this is the chief value of the voice critique and the proposal of other metaphors to replace the voice metaphor. Comparison and critique is the way we understand difference, and in our postmodern world, difference is a signifying act, enabling us to define practices and to understand the hegemonic nature of those practices.

Finally, although the metaphors I've suggested in this chapter come from feminist or women's studies, they should not be construed as being the exclusive domain of women. In other words, these metaphors constitute ways of viewing discourse, particularly written discourse, and while they differ from traditional perspectives that have dominated our culture (and consequently tended to be associated with the social group in control—white males), it would be fallacious to reason that these "other" perspectives are limited to women, since there are many marginalized social groups.

Chapter Seven

Networks: The Technological Disruption of Voice

Cyberfeminism

Sadie Plant, a lecturer in Cultural Studies at Birmingham University in the United Kingdom and more recently the founder of the Cybernetic Culture Research Unit at Warwick University, claims to have coined the term "cyberfeminism" to explain the developing connection or "alliance" between women and technology. She argues that there is considerable affinity between the way women work and think and the way modern computers operate, particularly the reliance on nonlinear associations and networks. Although computer users have thus far been predominately male, she asserts that the number of women who feel comfortable with electronic technology is rapidly increasing as women discover that learning to work using computers requires far less of a cognitive leap than they have been given to believe. (See Kozma 1966 and interviews with Plant in *New Statesmen and Society.*)

Given the technology phobias that have been socialized into women —many of whom have received information and technological training from men—it may take some time for women to be as comfortable with computers as Plant suggests. Nonetheless, the specific points of connection between women's ways of thinking and computers' ways of operating reveal much that is relevant to this voice critique. I want to focus particular attention on intuition, which has largely been regarded (and devalued) as a "female trait," but which figures importantly in the ways technology works. Often known as a sixth sense, intuition is a way of knowing that is difficult to describe. A person using her intuition is not relying on linear thinking or logical reasoning but rather on a

120

range of sensory faculties—seeing (perceiving), hearing, feeling, touching, even tasting—in order to know or to understand. These senses are used associatively, and are so intertwined that it is practically impossible for a person to identify "how" she knows something. It is not that she heard it or saw it or touched it (though in fact she may be doing all these); all she knows is that she has "sensed" it, and this lack of specificity contributes to its devaluation as legitimate knowledge, particularly in a world that values linear reasoning, explicitness, and precision as fundamental to knowing.

Speaking or listening—and their counterparts, writing and reading—have, in the history of philosophy, traditionally been associated with the formal acquisition of knowledge. We acquire knowledge from listening or reading; we know because we can think things through logically; we display (or share or refute) that knowledge through writing or speaking. Although computers began as logic machines to help speed up the process of thinking things through (especially things numerical), they have become increasingly complex not only in what they can handle but in how they can handle it. Interactive networks, multiple media, and interconnected information bytes and computational systems—in other words, webs of associated constituents—invite conceptions of knowledge and knowledge making that are quite different from the reading, writing, speaking, and listening paradigms that made voice possible. The interactive aspects of modern computer systems signal a shift away from linear and logical thinking and toward intuition; electronic constituents work on levels that are associative, layered, and multisensory. In fact, despite the fact that Artificial Intelligence (AI) experts and other computer gurus still often refer to intuition as "fuzzy logic," the idea of operating, communicating, reading, writing, and thinking in terms of these kinds of networks has become a mainstay of work in electronic technology. And, significantly, the network is, as I have shown in Chapter 6, also a very vital metaphor for the rhetoric of women.

Using this point of intersection between women's studies and computers as a place to start, this chapter will show how the use of voice in the electronic environment, because it relies narrowly on the connection between speech and writing for its explanatory power, explains and elucidates very little. I will explore what an electronic network entails—its character and nature—and investigate the important ramifications for using the networking metaphor in composition and rhetoric studies and teaching. Although my examples—given the nature of technology—can only be representative and will inevitably be out of date by the time this book is published, they will reinforce the central contention of this book, that voice has lost its currency as a valuable and useful metaphor.

The Environment of Electronic Technology

One of the reasons that electronic technology has such a prominent place in the world today is its capacity to accommodate, process, and produce large quantities of information—all kinds of information: verbal, visual, tactile, auditory, numeric, and symbolic. In Chapter 5, I discussed how print can conceivably convey a voice, how font styles (such as typeface, type size, italics, and boldface), underlining, punctuation, and syntax can provide cues to how written discourse is to be voiced. Different font typefaces, font styles, and font sizes can change from text to text or within a single text, conceivably translating into shifts in loudness, stress, or accent. Electronic writing, however, has the potential—a potential that has already been reached many times over—for conveying far more than the voice metaphor can sufficiently capture. Changes in style of the print (for example, ornate cursive versus computer graphic print), formatting, scrolling, color background or foreground, graphics, movement, embedded sounds, and the accumulation of windows on the computer screen can convey meaning that doesn't correspond to verbal communication. Although it is well beyond the scope of this chapter—and indeed this book—to discuss the multiple ways in which a visual or multisensory medium can signify,[1] I want to provide some representative examples to show how electronic writing projects construct meaning.

In a traditional text such as the one you are reading now—a text that consists primarily of printed words on a page with few graphics or illustrations—it is simply not possible to convey adequately the kinds of visual signification that typifies much of the current electronic technology. In printed books, readers often balk at the idea of interrupting the smooth flow of their reading by flipping pages around or redirecting their attention and may not be inclined to refer to illustrations, diagrams, or footnoted explanations located on another "distant" place or page. Electronic texts can avoid these kinds of problems with multiple screens and links that can be accessed immediately. It has become common to forecast the demise of the printed text, in part because of the clumsiness of reading texts (and writing them) in a world that craves speed and convenience. It might be preferable, in fact, to read (or view) this entire chapter (Chapter 7 of *The Mythology of Voice*) on a diskette so that the illustrations and examples I provide could be accessed electronically, giving the reader/viewer a more accurate sense of what I mean. But at this date, electronic books are only slowly making their way into the mainstream.

One electronic book, Jay Bolter's *Writing Space*, which explores the impact of electronic writing, is available both in hard copy and on diskette. Within certain parameters, readers can add to or modify the electronic text as they see fit. Electronic writing is also being used for literary studies, linking the analysis with examples to explore such things as the layering of meaning in a work of literature through links and multiple screens (also known as *hypertext*). Electronic texts are also frequently used in teaching. For example, at the Royal Melbourne Institute of Technology, students in a cinema studies class use hypertext software to write their analyses of films, incorporating still images and digitized video and sound into their "papers." Groups of students can link their projects together and these can potentially be tied to other sites outside the classroom. Among the advantages of this kind of writing is that students, in making their analyses, are able to avoid the tedious task of having to describe filmic images with language that can only summarize or approximate what is happening on the screen. Students also benefit from being able to isolate film clips that illustrate their points so that both writer/creator and the reader/viewer have the film clips in front of them as they read the discussion sections. Similar kinds of group-editing capabilities are available on a variety of software programs, including Microsoft for Windows.

While this book on voice remains in the traditional genre of an academic publication, I have, throughout this chapter, referenced material posted on the Boynton/Cook web site (at http://www.boyntoncook.com) that will provide a working example of some of the very basic elements I discuss here and with which I can demonstrate the real activity of the computer screen as I explain. For those readers without access to a computer or the Internet, or who prefer to simply read, I include reproductions in the text of some of the screens on the web tour. (For further information on viewing the web site material, please refer to the Appendix.)

Hypertext

For those unfamiliar with electronic writing, hypertext is a text on the computer screen that contains links to a particular computer environment, of which the World Wide Web is the best-known example. A hypertext link may be a word, a phrase, an icon or another symbol that, when clicked with a mouse, moves the viewer to another space or other spaces within the computer environment. Hypertext is, then, "extended" text and most often extends in sequences that are neither fixed nor chronological. The sample on the web contains a vastly simplified example of hypertext. In Screen #1 (shown in Figure 7–1), there is a row of buttons (hypertext links) that can be pressed to move a viewer from screen to screen or to exit. On subsequent screens, viewers are invited to click on buttons or icons to see examples of color, font, and audio.

Figure 7–1

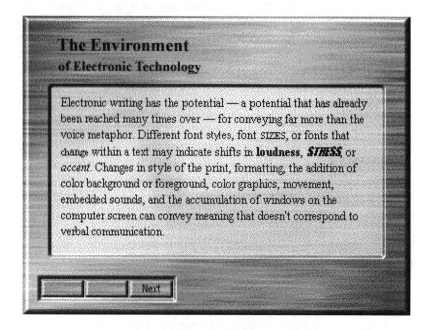

Hypertext is used for all kinds of different genres of electronic writing. For my discussion on voice, which is often associated with narrative (see Chapter 3), hypertext fiction provides some of the most telling examples of the inadequacies of the voice metaphor, and so I spend some time on it here.

Hypertext fiction begins with what looks to be an electronic version of a traditional text. It appears on the computer screen instead of on a white page. After the prefatory screens that explain the author's goals and instructions on ways of proceeding, each space usually contains a short passage within which are "hot" links—key words or phrases that, when clicked, open up other pages. Often these are not links to a "next" scene in the fictional narrative but to digressions, some of them fictional, some historical, others explanatory or illustrative.

Links can also be of infinite variety. They can be strictly textual—referring to other texts; they can contain quotations (such as from a poem by Arthur Rimbaud, a passage by a postmodern theorist, or a comment by a historian); they can introduce a new scene; or they can interject a commentary by the author on the story, the character, or the nature of hypertext itself. In one path through Carolyn Guyer's *Quibbling* (1992), a reader/viewer sees a screen in which a character states: "You know sometimes I can sing pretty well when no one is around." The words *I can sing* are linked to another screen, which reads,

"She sometimes sang 'O Salutaris' in the stairwells at work. The acoustics there thrilled her." *O Salutaris* is, in turn, linked to a screen containing the verses of the song in Latin, which is linked to an English translation. None of the links need to be followed, and each link has other links. Every story is, in a sense, layered with potential digressions, explanations, or other stories.

Links can contain visual elements like photographs, illustrations, labels, or screen graphics. Stuart Moulthrop's *Victory Garden* (1991), for example, at one point features a black screen that is linked to a white screen with a dot in the middle. In Michael Joyce's hypertext classic, *afternoon, a story* (1987), one of the links illustrates fragmentation: each screen in a series has a different word in a different position and location on the screen. Read chronologically, the words do not equal a sentence, and seem to be nonsense (a result of fragmentation), but if the reader continues to move to the next screen, he will eventually be lead back to the initial link. Some hypertext links have this kind of circularity; many do not.

Most hypertext authors provide a map, which serves to chart where the viewer has been, as well as a screen that serves as a guide to how elements are linked. Sometimes the authors have programmed these links so that viewers' routes are limited; sometimes the routes are given a hierarchical structure. But most frequently, the reader is the author of her journey through the hypertexts, or, more precisely, the author of her "reading."

Hypertext fiction can be read without following the links by simply reading a screen and moving to the next in what appears to be an order. But the purpose of hypertext fiction is to allow for digressions and "creative" reading. With its links and interconnections, hypertext works to disrupt a chronological or linear reading and allows the reader to pursue multiple routes through the text in whatever order she would like, even to the extent of following links to texts written or "generated" by different authors.

It is difficult to determine precise beginnings and endings. Joyce's *afternoon* begins with a preface in which he comments on the problem of closure. The next screen, labeled "Afternoon, a story — [begin]" reads:

> I try to recall winter. <As if it were yesterday?> she says, but I do not signify one way or another.

We seem to encounter a story *in media res*, and there are immediate links, contributing to a sense of frenetic activity on the part of both reader (who must figure out who the characters are, what the scene is, and what's going on in order to understand) and the writer, who has programmed in all kinds of layers that can be immediately accessed. Some of the links will answer questions, such as who "she" is, but most links will elicit more questions. Thus we are given to understand that there is no "best place" to begin, but rather that we have to make our own way to understanding.

A sense of closure is indeed impossible and is only effected when the reader decides to log off, perhaps quitting with an unsettling sense of ambiguity, "Did I finish?" "What did I miss?" "Did the author intend to end it somewhere? If so, where?" In other words, the process forces the reader into a postmodern reading of the "story," one that is discontinuous, ambiguous, and indeterminate. Some of the links in Moulthrop's *Victory Garden* lead to dead ends; the reader is forced to return to previous screens to find a way to continue. And, where links lead to screens the viewer has seen before, often the screens that follow are different the second (or third or fourth or fifth) time around. One could conceivably argue that the author has some control over this in the ways it has been constructed, and that the reader has some power—the power of selection—but ultimately, the entire act of reading is a chaotic and often disjointed melding of texts, readings, and intentions. In hypertext fiction, control is illusory and hence the feeling of disruption or disorder.

Part of the disruption comes from the instability of each word or phrase. In *afternoon,* each word in nearly every passage has a link (or is part of a link) to another part of the text; thus each word is "loaded" with potential meanings or senses in a way that is not possible in print. In his introductory screen, Joyce celebrates this quality and refers to it as "yielding." Linked words yield in both senses of *yield:* they submit to the touch, and they produce a surplus value. The meaning of words then is not only loaded with potential meaning from the links, but fluid (a metaphor also used in women's studies, described in the previous chapter), where a word can mean one thing in one context and then, as the link is opened up, the same word can acquire other connotations. Joyce invites the reader to read "inquisitively" or "playfully." And indeed, reading hypertext fiction is much like playing a game, with its icons, snatches of dialogue, story fragments, multiple images, and freedom of movement.

Interestingly, a text of this kind asks the reader to focus special attention on form, format, and language as she determines what links to pursue. Christopher Keep and Tim McLaughlin (1995) point out in their web review of *afternoon* (a review that also contains links) that this attention tends to defamiliarize the text, shifting the focus from the meaning that the language conveys to the language itself and, in so doing, tends to frustrate any definitive reading. Definitive reading is frustrated for sure, but not in the sense of defamiliarization meant by Keep, McLaughlin, or the Russian formalists. The reader does not necessarily slow down and linger on the individual words or expressions in the process of making sense. If anything, hypertext links speed up reading as readers—with a single mouse click—move from one link to another, both forwards or backwards. It is this rapid shifting of contexts and connotations that contributes to the sense of play as well as to the potential for different ways of knowing, ones that are fragmented, changeable, and fluid.

One could argue, at least at this point in time when the technology is relatively new, that the reader must pay considerable attention to the language of hypertext. Hypertext features an array of icons at the top or bottom of every screen, denoting possible moves or particular connections. While the readers/viewers may, on one level, pay attention to the style of language in the conventional sense, they are also paying attention to the technology: to the ways things (words and images) appear on the screen; to how links are called up; or to what decisions to make. Should, for example, a reader follow this link or that one? Go back to the map and see where to go or where he has been? Get an overview as to what lies ahead? Choice involves weighing options, making determinations based on a myriad of considerations, and a reader cannot help but wonder about the road not taken.

Electronic Signification

In addition to hypertext, there is a myriad of other ways computers signify. To restate the obvious, print consists of black-and-white symbols on a white page. Signification comes through the decoding of those symbols and is further affected by conventions such as formatting (margins and headers, for example), type font, and conventions such as punctuation, sentencing, paragraphs, chapters, indices, and appendices (see the discussion in Chapter 5). The computer medium seems to start with the conventions, then breaks them in what seems to be an ongoing quest not simply for novelty, but to make optimal use of the medium for enhanced impact on the reader/viewer. With electronic writing we are seeing an enormous amount of experimentation and a lively sense of play, typified not just by the proliferation of computer games, but also by a whole range of maneuverable graphical features that invite the reader/viewer to take part. The result is often a bombardment of multimedia stimuli, the consequences of which we are only beginning to assess. Recent interest in visual literacy as a way to engage students and as a subject of study is a result, at least in part, of electronic writing. The annual Conference on College Composition and Communication already has a number of sessions each year that are devoted to visual literacy; these sessions invite teachers to take advantage of the sophisticated visual awareness that students bring to the classroom from hours spent watching television, videos, and computer screens. Theorists such as Gunther Kress and Theo van Leeuwen (1996) are investigating ways that the visual medium signifies and will provide valu-

Figure 7–2

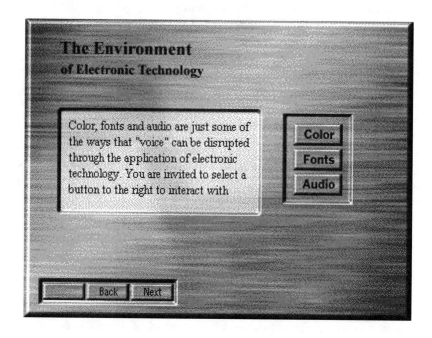

able information to professional and nonprofessional creators of software and web pages.

The following is a representative sampling of some of the signifying features of electronic writing that cannot be adequately addressed using voice. The sample on the web site (also illustrated in hard copy in Figures 7–1 through 7–6) is an electronic demonstration of some of these elements. The screen shown in Figure 7–2 introduces the elements (fonts, color, and audio), then invites you to interact.

Fonts and Formats

Fonts, including symbol, size, shape, and intensity, are infinitely variable in the electronic environment (see Figure 7–3). The font style can change as it is viewed. Typeface can be animated, curvilinear, handwritten; it can pop off and on the screen. New symbols are constantly being created and developed, and this includes the proliferation of screen icons to represent available options (print, save, trash, reply, etc.). The possibilities are currently limited only by how usable and functional the features are deemed to be (by creator and user).

Format, as well, has limitless possibilities. Screens with traditionally printed text can be altered in any number of ways, including

Figure 7–3

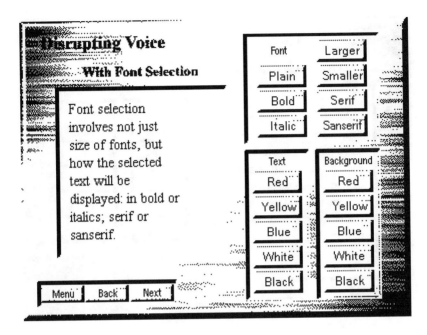

adjusting margins, columns, direction, motion, and location of print. Scrolling also adds to effect of movement and can also affect reading speed, order, and perception. Perhaps the most interesting formatting possibilities are nonprint visuals and graphics, which communicate and express a range of moods, feelings, and ideas.

Color

We already know quite a bit about how strongly color affects human response. It impacts mood, feelings, and emotions, and has a documented effect upon brain waves, the nervous system, and hormonal activity. Color influences the estimation of volume, motion, time, temperature, and noise. When a person is exposed to a given color, for as little as five minutes, his mental, as well as muscular, activity changes. Color can be used to stimulate, depress, relax, cheer, invigorate, or irritate, and it can cause actual physical discomfort.

In his series on color in design, Dale Russell (1990) explores the effects of different colors. Red, he points out, is highly charged and emotional, having the capability to increase hormonal or sexual activity and to heal wounds. Yellow is moody, the color both of health (sunshine) and illness (jaundice). Teal creates a sense of sophistication, and so on.

Figure 7–4

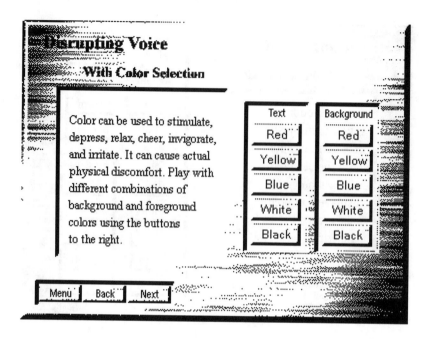

One color, when used in juxtaposition with another color, changes the hue and texture, resulting in changes in effect on the viewer.

In the computer environment, not only can the background have color, it can also have multiple colors that can change quickly (see Figure 7–4). The foreground (print, graphics, etc.) can have color as well, and the relationship between foreground and background colors can add another dimension of affect. Furthermore, the viewer can change these colors, changing the visual effect, and hence, the impact.

Color works intuitively, influencing multiple senses and resulting in a message that—much like voice—is hard to pin down. And it is, of course, a visual stimulus, not an aural one, and consequently invites response from sensory faculties that cannot be represented in the voice metaphor.

Audio

In addition to visual components, computers are capable of highly so-phisticated audio features (see Figure 7–5), enhanced by components such as CD-ROM. Examples of audio include music, voice-over, and sound effects. Because a viewer accesses these tactically (by clicking a mouse) and visually (by viewing the screen), the effect works at a range

Figure 7–5

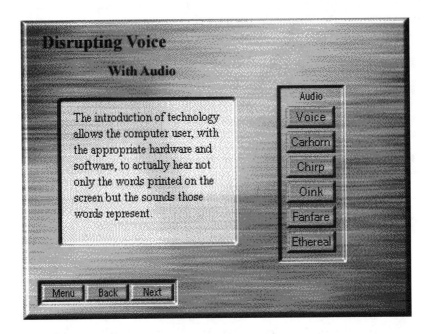

of overlapping sensory levels. A viewer is looking at what is happening on the screen, seeing the effect of moving one's fingers to click the mouse or move the icon, and hearing what the video provides. The audio may work in conjunction with the visual and the tactile, or it may serve as a counterpoint or a mood analogue.

Video

Before long, most computer systems will be capable of replaying video, combining the audio and the visual on screen in ways that can be manipulated, allowing the viewer to freeze-frame, edit, fast forward, decelerate to slow motion, even add or create images—enabling the computer operator to become both creator and viewer.

At this moment in time, the culmination of multimedia capabilities is computer-animated virtual reality, where, with a helmet apparatus consisting of special glasses and headphones, a pair of gloves, and a willingness to travel, a person can have the sensation of being transported into another world. Here sensation plays a crucial role. A viewer can see and hear, but he can also touch, feeling contours, textures, and shapes; he can even feel pain. And he can change the environment, interacting with it by conversing with characters (or killing or healing them) or creating elements (or destroying them). There is also the potential for the disruption of time as we know it, as virtual reality has the capability for speeding up time or slowing it down. We currently use virtual reality mostly for training simulation (in flight training, for example) or games; we have barely begun to explore it.

Implications for Voice

Among the key distinctions between electronic texts and traditional texts that I hope have become apparent from the preceding sections are:

1. Electronic texts communicate much more than the verbal. As Bolter (1991) writes,

   Electronic writing is both a visual and a verbal description. It is not the writing of a place, but rather a writing *with* places, spatially realized topics. Topographic writing challenges the idea that writing should be merely the servant of spoken language. The writer and reader can create and examine signs and structures on the computer screen that have no easy equivalent in speech. (25)

   Add to this sound effects, audio-visual components, and tactile stimuli and you have a multisensory environment.

2. There is no consistent central control. Electronic writing takes place at multiple levels and dimensions. As a consequence, it is non-linear; there is no closure. A user can go on and on and on.

3. Users can engage in what Plant calls "identity hacking." That is, they can develop multiple personae, going online as a male, female, anyone at all, or no one. As a result, the distinctions between writer, reader, student, teacher, professional, and novice are not as clear as they are with print.

4. Electronic writing involves the disruption of our standard assumptions about time, texts, reading, and response. Cyberspace offers the opportunity to exchange written ideas in real time—a concept that has ramifications for academic journals, essays, books, and student papers. With immediate feedback and response, the notion of permanence is jeopardized—for good or ill; everything one writes is immediately revisable by the originating writer or by her multiple readers—who may be distant in both space and time.

As I have argued in earlier chapters, the voice metaphor is contingent upon certain suppositions about authorship, linearity, and stability, and it relies upon the strong relationship between orality and literacy. To illustrate how voice no longer applies in an electronic environment, I want to explore more fully the ramifications I listed here.

Authorship and the Individual Voice

With hypertext we see, once again, how the concept of authorship be-comes a difficult one to sustain. An "author" may (a) write the text; (b) generate the visuals; (c) select the hypertext software; (d) create the links; and (e) define the often multiple ways in which a text can be read or the links followed, controlling to some extent the routes a reader or viewer can take. One might also argue that readers could get a sense of an authorial voice or a sense of an author's special style in the short written passages that appear in a single screen. But much of the mate-rial that a reader can read or access through a hypertext is not "au-thored" by one individual, nor does it seem like it is, although an author's name (Joyce, Guyer, Moulthrop) may be still attached to the work as a whole—both as a matter of convention and for traditional copyright purposes, which still apply almost anachronistically to this new medium. As we have seen, voice depends upon the reader's abil-ity to identify a coherent "persona." But in fact, a reader may not get a sense about the identity of a controlling "voice" at all, and the originat-ing author—the one who "composed" or put the work and language into play—has far less ability to fashion a "voice," given the multiple ways hypertext can be read or experienced. *Victory Garden* contains a feature that allows the reader to make margin notations that he can call up during a future reading, so that the reader's annotation becomes a permanent part of his subsequent readings, making the reader's contri-bution literally "present" on the screen, and putting him in a position of being the author of his reading.

In an attempt to put hypertext in perspective, Jay Bolter explains that traditional print media

> tended to magnify the distance between the author and the reader, as the author became a monumental figure, the reader only a visitor in the author's cathedral. Electronic writing emphasizes the imperma-nence and changeability of text, and it tends to reduce the distance be-tween author and reader by turning the reader into an author. (3)

But the reader is only one of many authors, and increasingly the con-trolling author in an electronic text becomes so difficult to determine or to maintain that he or she becomes relatively unimportant. Author-ship is an artifact of print; electronic writing may force us to place the emphasis of study elsewhere, and not on the author or the speaker in the text, all of which validate Foucault's well-known pronounce-ments about the fate of the authors in "What Is an Author" (see my Chapter 4 for discussion).

> We should no longer hear the questions that have been rehashed for so long: "Who really spoke? Is it really he and not someone else? . . .

Instead, there would be other questions like these: "What are the modes of existence of this discourse? Where has it been used, how can it circulate, and who can appropriate it for himself? . . . And behind all these questions we would hear hardly anything but the stirring of an indifference: "What difference does it make who is speaking?" (160)

The idea of a singular text emanating from a single individual or having a single voice is a concept that will not die easily, entrenched as it is in Western thought (for more comprehensive discussions, see Lunsford and Ede [1990]; Woodmansee and Jaszi [1994]). It may well be that the forces of postmodernism, feminism, and multiculturalism won't be sufficient to dislodge the epistemologies favored by the status quo. But electronic writing, because it deals with a new and powerful medium, will surely compel us to adjust our ways of knowing, communicating, and expressing. Already we may be moved to consider what Carolyn Guyer, in the one of the screens in her hypertext novel, *Quibbling*, contemplates:

What if it becomes so that there are no more singular works? That is, the connections among everything (OK, let's just keep it to "literature" for now—the connections among all writing) become instantiated to the point that a focus of any kind is like using a microscope, or maybe like visiting a cove, or walking through a puddle. The point is that when everything is connected and we can see or get a sense of how that is, then the individual, singular (person, event, thing) becomes even clearer against it. Or within it? It's when we isolate, divide, exclude in order to emphasize the individual that we really lose what we are after. The individual alone and unconnected is disappeared into the black hole for things that don't exist. (Screen "figure/ground")

If we persist in searching for a voice in texts and in championing the notion of stylistic integrity that makes voice possible, then we will surely be outsiders to a technological world.

Textual Unity

With the fragmentation of authorship and the reader's perception of a cohesive textual persona, which are so important to the notion of voice, comes the disruption of the unified narrative. A narrative, by its nature as a story, tends toward a kind of linearity, a working from event to event. Linearity is at risk in electronic writing because although the links provide the kind of cohesion that makes traditional linear narratives possible, electronic texts exist in multiple dimensions, which the reader can access at any time and in multiple spaces. Voice depends upon a certain integrity to make it identifiable and distinguishable from other voices; voice depends upon difference. If integrity is imperiled with electronic writing, then unity, the working of all parts as one, will be as well because it relies on the idea of control: a controlling presence or a controlling "author." The fragmented character of the electronic environment means, as Bolter points out, that electronic texts are "in a perpetual state of reorganization" (9). Reminiscent of Bakhtin's centrifugal and centripetal distinctions (see Chapter 4), Bolter believes this force to reorganize (to unify), which fights the forces of fragmentation, leads to a new kind of unity. But I would argue that it is likely that what we have traditionally understood as unity is no longer possible or even desirable. Unity, a concept reminiscent of a logocentrism criticized by postmodernists, is even more temporary and illusory in electronic texts than it is in traditional texts; even an electronic text that begins as a linear narrative is perpetually undermined by the mechanics of hypertext, by the next person logging on, or some other preprogrammed or newly programmed thread (again a "texture" metaphor) or visual. While interrupted and nonlinear narratives are nothing new in literature where flashbacks, flash-forwards, leaps in time, and other disjunctions are common, in nonliterary texts, these devices rarely exist. By contrast, electronic writing (fiction or nonfiction) has radiating signification and leaps in space, making it troublesome to summarize even the most "informational" of texts and impossible to reduce them to a unified whole.

The Virus as Metaphor and Other Destablizers

Computer viruses—created by techno-felons of electronic writing to disrupt computer operations and information storage and retrieval—reinforce how vulnerable the sense of stability is in an electronic environment. Stability, which characterizes our sense of print—because print conveys the impression of permanence, hence stable meaning—makes possible the perception that when we write, our intentions (as well as our voice, or at least a voice) are being conveyed to (or heard by) the reader. But in addition to the already variable nature of the electronic world, viruses are affronts to intentionality, which is already at risk through multiple readers, readings, and media.

There are other disruptions. Often electronic listservs or newsgroups are set up to enable subscribers to share information, air their views, and discuss issues. But even those listservs that specify procedures and online etiquette (netiquette) in attempts to encourage serious (consistent, extended, attentive to the rules of that discourse) electronic dialogue about issues, are persistently undermined by playfulness, flaming (harassing), spamming (jamming), and interloping—that is, by people not belonging to the discourse—disturbing what we in academia understand by "productive" dialogue, a term that depends upon an agreement about what productive dialogue entails. Even when everybody who subscribes to a list knows and obeys the rules, a virus may come along and wipe out the software. Electronic writing is precarious, delicate, unstable, and wholly unreliable, and that is, ironically, what can make it valuable as a means of expression and communication—as a "language." If applied linguists have taught us anything in the past twenty years, it is that language is not particularly stable; in fact, *change* is the only linguistic constant. As a means of communication, it is capricious and untrustworthy; too many variables stemming from contexts of use and the diversity, moods, goals, and personalities of its users influence every language endeavor. While we must believe otherwise when we converse, language involves misunderstanding more than understanding, and that for many linguists (and certainly for literary critics) is what makes it so exciting to study.

Intuition and New Metaphors

We have seen how difficult it is to sustain the idea of a controlling textual persona in cyberspace. But while electronic technology will undoubtedly affect how we perceive ourselves and our texts—much like the use of print did when it became widespread—the impact and influence of the printed word is still formidable today. Print literacy is embedded in our culture; thus even when we use electronic media, it is difficult to subscribe immediately to alternative ways of perceiving ourselves and our relationships with our texts. But I would argue that attempting to understand the world of texts in terms of networks rather than voices can provide insights into how we exist in the world: how our responses are networked to the utterances of others (a Bakhtinian concept); how we express, communicate, inform, persuade, and exist in contexts that include color, shape, movement, texture—all of which are revealed by the senses; and, finally, how the power of language goes significantly beyond what voice can convey.

Some people (voice proponents among them) argue that it is our voice (ability to speak or "express ourselves" in language) that makes us human. I would argue that this is the narrow view. What makes us human is the ability to understand that we are enmeshed in a world, one that includes not just humans as individuals, but physical, mental, psychic, and metaphysical dimensions of living and nonliving forms, of nature, and of matter. We are linked not only by the ability to hear, acknowledge, and respond to one another's voices but also by our ability to touch, see, feel, and intuit.

The network metaphor, borrowed both from electronic technology and from women's studies, expresses well these interconnections. Using a network as a metaphorical scheme instead of voice might enable us to honor intuitive knowledge, to emphasize links, contexts, and movement rather than authors, individual selves, and textual unity. Electronic technology not only invites us to participate as linked, multisensory beings, but demands it.

While the network metaphor does not make the rhetorical manipulation as overt or clear as it might be if one conceived of a text as a web, there are several advantages in conceptualizing texts in terms of networks. First, a network seems better suited than the web to avoiding the problem of being overshadowed by its creator. The web may always carry with it strong connections to its weaver (spider); the design of a web may be a reflection of the idiosyncrasies of its creator. As a result, it can also be easily conceived of as being owned, and this may be important and have consequences. By contrast, the network is always the construction of numerous parties and hence cannot convey a character except by collusion or mutual agreement.

Second, a tear or break in the network doesn't necessarily mean disaster in the same sense as it might mean in the web. Networks are usually quite easy to reconfigure, and—especially in electronic networks—change is not only constant but also desirable. Flexibility is a valuable characteristic of a network. Certainly webs have some ability to bend and reshape themselves, but they are also quite fragile and can be easily damaged beyond repair.

If a student understands her writing in terms of a network, she may readily see the interconnections of words, sentences, paragraphs, and white space within it, and the correlation between those elements and (1) other texts; (2) her audience(s)—intended and otherwise; (3) other intentions, purposes, forces within the world. She will not see the promotion of her own voice as the necessary goal; rather, she will be able to work on strengthening the interconnections or forging new ones before her text is "set loose." This may mean she will want to understand how a certain term she uses has a number of different connotations or "senses" according to who reads it. Or it may mean she'll want to consider other rhetorical choices (for example, emotive language) to counter the rational argument that may have typified another well-known paper on the same topic.

Third, perceiving texts, writing, and authoring in terms of a network extends our work in the composition course well beyond the practice of reading and writing. Jim Gee frequently talks about understanding literacy in terms of Discourse with a capital D, that is, as ways of being in the world, not limited to reading, writing, speaking, listening, but including behaving, thinking, arguing, and knowing. It's a complex of practices, related to culture, ethnicity, gender, power, status, and wealth. If teachers and students of rhetoric perceive the world in terms of a network or a web or an embrace, then they might more quickly and insightfully come to understand what rhetoric is and does. As a result, they might see themselves in situations where they can indeed question the social and linguistic apparatuses that control and shape their lives.

Note

1. See, for example, Kress and van Leeuwen 1996.

Epilogue

I have attempted a study of tremendous scope in this book, and I don't pretend to have done justice either to the breadth or depth of material; obviously, much more can and should be said about voice. There are few metaphors as powerful or as embedded in our rhetorical consciousness and national value system. I suspect, too, that there are probably metaphors other than the ones I have promoted in this book that might be suitable alternatives to voice. I only hope to have demonstrated the kinds of questions and responses that should figure as part of a discussion not only of voice but also of the language we use to discuss writing.

By way of conclusion, I want to raise a final issue that has figured largely in the preceding discussion, but that strikes me as insufficiently addressed. The issue has to do with the interconnection between postmodernism—the tenets of which underlie much of my thesis—and, for lack of a better term, alternative or "multicultural" rhetorics. I have discussed alternative rhetorics only in passing, which is not an indication of any lack of importance but rather of the tremendous scope, for alternative rhetorics offer a variety of remarkable options for ways to consider text. To many educators, postmodernism seems both unappealing and threatening, primarily because deconstructing texts, ideas, and environments ostensibly results in anarchy—taking an idea apart for its own sake without putting something back in its place. But postmodernism, while seemingly anarchic, does not champion chaos; rather, postmodernists undertake the continued questioning of structures and the breaking apart of networks as an invitation to reestablish them, however tentatively.

Rhetorics that serve as alternatives to American dominant discourse often come from marginalized social groups (among them African Americans, Asians, Hispanics, and women). These groups seem to understand, at least tacitly, the connection between deconstruction and networks within which change and difference are celebrated. Berenice Reagon (1995), founding member of the a capella group "Sweet Honey in the Weave" and a promoter of African American oral traditions, suggests that the way to understand the African American is to understand the importance of change and diversity. Both potentially undermine the status quo because, by definition, the status quo is averse to change; control and stability are key to maintaining monolithic cultural institutions. But subverting the status quo is not as much the goal of this oral society as espousing and understanding alternative cultural values. The idea behind the African American oral tradition, she argues, is that you don't make sounds by yourself; rather, you and others come together, and everyone draws on the group. To do so, you must give up any primary allegiance to yourself as a self-sufficient individual. "If you don't have humility," she maintains, "you don't survive the journey that is the African American experience." By the same token, coming together does not necessarily create harmony. Singing in a group that pieces itself together from a network of assorted and divergent experiences results in songs that are raspy, angry, joyful, energetic, and tired, sometimes all at once. And that is the beauty of collective participation. As Reagon puts it: "Even when we're smoothing, there's texture in the weave" (1994, 14). In a sense, we can perceive the tradition as a network in which we see the array of components that constitute the network itself.

Network metaphors are particularly appropriate in the rhetorics of a variety of other cultures, which unfortunately are often devalued within the American mainstream, despite our revolutionary, multicultural beginnings. Networks may be useful ways of looking, for example, at the Native American's sense of oneness with the past, present, and future and his complex relationship with the natural world. The network metaphor might also help us understand the Asian emphasis on deferral of ego in which the self is indeterminate and personal identity is not necessarily the same as the individual person. For example, the Japanese notion of *migawari* (surrogation), which Taki Sugiyama Lebra calls the "cultural idiom of self-exchange," seems to rely on boundaries between the self and the social that are quite fluid (qtd. in Ames 1994, 107–123). This is also true in Chinese Confucianism, which espouses the notion that learning to be human is discovering how to be sensitive to an ever-expanding network of relationships. (For representative studies, see Ames 1994, Solomon 1994, and Allen 1983.)

Whatever language we use to describe how we think and write ultimately comes down to what we value, making the whole issue both highly political and highly personal. That is why voice is so important to understand and question, and why is it not only useful but desirable to question regularly metaphors that are so firmly entrenched in our lexicons. We come to understand thereby a bit more about ourselves.

Works Cited

Adams, H., ed. 1971. *Critical Theory Since Plato.* San Diego: Harcourt Brace Jovanovich.

Allen, P. G. 1983. *Studies in American Indian Literature.* New York: MLA.

Ames, R. T., with W. Dissanayke and T. P. Kasulis. 1994. *Self as Person in Asian Theory and Practice.* Albany: State University of New York Press.

Ansen, D. 1996. "When America Lost Its Innocence—Maybe." Eds. R. B. Axelrod and C. R. Cooper. *Reading Critically, Writing Well.* New York: St. Martin's Press.

Applebee, A. N. 1974. *Tradition and Reform in the Teaching of English: A History.* Urbana, IL: NCTE.

Aristotle. 1982. *The "Art" of Rhetoric,* Vol. 22. Trans. J. H. Freese. Cambridge, MA: Harvard University Press.

Atwood, M. 1989. *Bodily Harm.* New York: Bantam.

Austen, J. [1816] 1957. *Emma.* Boston: Houghton Mifflin.

Axelrod, R. B., and C. R. Cooper. 1996. *Reading Critically, Writing Well.* New York: St. Martin's Press.

Baddeley, A. 1986. *Working Memory.* Oxford, UK: Clarendon Press.

Baev, B. 1957. *On Certain Peculiarities of Inner Speech in Mental Problem Solving of Various Types* (PAN No.3). Moscow: Dolk.

Baker, S. [1972, 1966] 1976. *The Complete Stylist and Handbook.* New York: Thomas Y. Crowell Company.

———. 1976. *The Practical Stylist.* New York: Harper and Row.

Bakhtin, M. 1981. *The Dialogic Imagination.* Ed. M. Holquist. Trans. C. Emerson and M. Holquist. Austin: University of Texas Press.

———. 1986. *Speech Genres & Other Late Essays.* Ed. C. Emerson and M. Holquist. Trans. V. W. McGee. Austin: University of Texas Press.

Bates, S. 1996. "Religious Diversity and the Schools." Eds. R. B. Axelrod and C. R. Cooper. *Reading Critically, Writing Well.* New York: St. Martin's Press.

Bateson, G. 1955. "The Message 'This Is Play.'" In *Group Processes.* Ed. B. Schaffner. New York: Josiah Macy, Jr., Foundation Proceedings.

Belenky, M. F., B. M. Clinchy, N. R. Goldberger, and J. M. Tarule. 1986. *Women's Ways of Knowing: The Development of Self, Voice and Mind.* New York: Basic Books.

Berlin, J. A. 1987. *Rhetoric and Reality: Writing Instruction in American Colleges, 1900–1985.* Carbondale: Southern Illinois University Press.

———. 1984. *Writing Instruction in Nineteenth-Century American Colleges.* Carbondale: Southern Illinois University Press.

Bettelheim, B. 1976. *The Uses of Enchantment.* New York: Knopf.

Bolinger, D. 1986. *Intonation and Its Parts: Melody in Spoken English.* Stanford, CA: Stanford University Press.

Bolter, J. D. 1991. *Writing Space: The Computer, Hypertext, and the History of Writing.* Hillsdale, NJ: Erlbaum.

Booth, W. 1961. *The Rhetoric of Fiction.* Chicago and London: University of Chicago Press.

Bowden, D. 1993. "The Limits of Containment in Composition Studies." *College Composition and Communication* 44.3: 364–379.

Brooks, C., and R. P. Warren. 1949. *Modern Rhetoric.* New York: Harcourt Brace & World.

Bulwer, J. [1644] 1974. *Chirologia: or the Natural Language of the Hand.* Ed. J. W. Cleary. Carbondale and Edwardsville: Southern Illinois University Press.

Burke, K. 1969. *A Grammar of Motives.* Berkeley: University of California Press.

Chafe, W. 1980. "The Deployment of Consciousness in the Production of Narrative." In *The Pear Stories: Cognitive, Cultural, and Linguistics Aspects of Narrative Production.* Ed. W. Chafe. Norwood, NJ: Ablex.

———. 1988. "Punctuation and the Prosody of Written Language." *Written Communication* 5.4 (October): 395–426.

Chatman, S. 1990. *Coming to Terms: The Rhetoric of Narrative in Fiction and Film.* Ithaca, New York: Cornell University Press.

Cherry, R. 1994. "Ethos Versus Persona: Self-Representation in Written Discourse." Ed. P. Elbow. *Landmark Essays on Voice and Writing.* Davis, CA: Hermagorus.

Childs, J. L. 1950. *Education and Morals.* New York: Appleton-Century-Crofts.

Cibber, C. 1970. *Apology for His Life.* Excerpted in *Actors on Acting.* Eds. T. Cole and H. K. Chinoy. New York: Crown Publishers.

Cixous, H. 1980. "The Laugh of the Medusa." Eds. E. Marks and I. de Courtivron. *New French Feminisms.* Amherst: University of Massachusetts Press.

Coles, W. E., Jr. 1983. *Composing: Writing as a Self-Creating Process.* Portsmouth, NH: Boynton/Cook.

———. [1978] 1988. *The Plural I.* Portsmouth, NH: Heinemann-Boynton/Cook.

Connors, R. J. 1987. "Personal Writing Assignments." *College Composition and Communication* 38.2 (May): 166–183.

Conrad, R. 1972. "Speech and Reading." In *Language by Ear and Eye.* Eds. J. Kavanaugh and I. Mattingly. Cambridge, MA: MIT Press.

Corbin, R. K., and P. G. Perrin. 1955. *Guide to Modern English.* Chicago: Scott, Foresman.

Coulmas, F. 1986. "Reported Speech: Some General Issues." In *Direct and Indirect Speech*. Ed. F. Coulmas. New York, Amsterdam: Mouton de Gruyter.

Crevecoeur, H. St. John de. [1782] 1904. *Letters from an American Farmer*. New York: Fox, Duffield and Co.

Dean, P. 1990. "The Paper Chase." *Los Angeles Times*, View Section, Dec. 4. E-1, 7.

Derrida, J. 1976. *Of Grammatology*. Trans. G. C. Spivak. Baltimore and London: The Johns Hopkins University Press.

———. 1973. *Speech and Phenomena and Other Essays on Husserl's Theory of Signs*. Trans. D. B. Allison. Evanston, IL: Northwestern University Press.

di Somi, L. [1556–1565] 1970. *Dialogues on State Affairs*. Excerpted in *Actors on Acting*. Eds. T. Cole and H. K. Chinoy. New York: Crown Publishers.

Dixon, John. 1967. *Growth Through English: A Report Based on the Dartmouth Seminar 1966*. Oxford, UK: Oxford University Press.

Ede, L. 1989. *Work in Progress: A Guide to Writing and Revising*. New York: St. Martin's Press.

Edfelt, A. 1960. *Silent Speech and Silent Reading*. Chicago: University of Chicago Press.

Eisenstein, E. 1980. *The Printing Press as an Agent of Change: Communications and Cultural Transformation in Early-Modern Europe*. Cambridge, UK: Cambridge University Press.

Elbow, P. 1986. *Embracing Contraries: Explorations in Learning and Teaching*. New York: Oxford University Press.

———. 1981. *Writing with Power*. New York and Oxford: Oxford University Press.

———. 1973. *Writing Without Teachers*. Oxford, UK: Oxford University Press.

———, ed. 1994. *Landmark Essays on Voice and Writing*. Davis, CA: Hermagoras.

Eliot, T. S. 1943. "The Three Voices of Poetry." *On Poetry and Poets*. New York: Farrar, Strauss & Cudahy.

Ellsworth, E. 1989. "Why Doesn't This Feel Empowering? Working Through the Repressive Myths of Critical Pedagogy." *Harvard Educational Review* 59.3: 297–324.

Emerson, R. W. 1960. *Selections from Ralph Waldo Emerson*. Ed. S. E. Whicher. Boston: Houghton Mifflin.

Faabourg-Anderson K., and A. Edfelt. 1958. "Electromography of Intrinsic and Extrinsic Laryngeal Muscles During Silent Speech: Correlations with Reading Activity. *Acta-Oto-Laryngology* 49: 478–482.

Faigley, L. 1986. "Competing Theories of Process: A Critique and a Proposal." *College English* 48.6: 527–542.

Farmer, F. 1995. "Voice Reprised: Dialogic Understanding." *Rhetoric Review* 13.2: 304–320.

Fish, S. 1980. "What is Stylistics." *Is There a Text in This Class?* Cambridge, MA: Harvard University Press.

Foucault, M. 1972. *The Archaeology of Knowledge and The Discourse on Language.* Trans. A. M. Sheridan Smith. New York: Pantheon.

———. 1977. *Language, Counter-Memory, Practice.* Trans. D. Bouchard and S. Simon. Ithaca, NY: Cornell University Press.

Franklin, B. [1771] 1961. *The Autobiography and Other Writings.* New York: New American Library (Signet Classic).

Fulkerson, R. 1979. "Four Philosophies of Composition." *College Composition and Communication* 30: 344–348.

Fulwiler, T. 1990. "Looking and Listening for My Voice." Staffroom Interchange. *CCC* 41.2 (May): 214–220.

Gadamer, H.-G. 1986. *The Relevance of the Beautiful and Other Essays.* Trans. N. Walker. Cambridge, UK: Cambridge University Press.

Gaines, R. J., J. Mandler, and P. Bryant. 1981. "Immediate and Delayed Story Recall by Hearing and Deaf Children." *Journal of Speech and Hearing Research* 24: 463–469.

Gee, J. P. 1989. "The Legacies of Literacy: From Plato to Freire through Harvey Graff." *Journal of Education* 171.1: 147–165.

———. 1989. "Self, Society, Mushfake, and Vygotsky: Meditations on Papers Redefining the Social in Composition Theory." *The Writing Instructor* 8.4: 177–183.

Genette, G. 1987. *Narrative Discourse: An Essay in Method.* Trans. J. E. Lewin. Ithaca, NY: Cornell University Press.

Gibson, W. 1969. *Persona: A Style Study for Readers and Writers.* New York: Random House.

———. 1962. "The Voice of the Writer." *College Composition and Communication* 8.3: 10–13.

Gilligan, C. 1982. *In a Different Voice: Psychological Theory and Women's Development.* Cambridge, MA: Harvard University Press.

Goffman, E. 1959. *The Presentation of Self in Everyday Life.* New York: Doubleday.

Goodman, N. 1978. *Ways of Worldmaking.* Indianapolis: Hackett Publishing Company.

Goodwin, C. 1984. "Notes on Story Structure and the Organization of Participation." In *Structures of Social Action.* Eds. M. Atkinson and J. Heritage. Cambridge, UK: Cambridge University Press.

Gould, S. J. 1989. *Wonderful Life: The Burgess Shale and the Nature of History.* New York: W. W. Norton & Co.

Guyer, C. 1992. *Quibbling.* (Hypertext Fiction). Watertown, MA: Eastgate Systems.

Halle, M., and K. Stevens. 1962. "Speech Recognition: A Model and a Program for Research." *IRE Transaction of the Professional Group on Information Theory* IT-8: 155–159.

Halloran, S. M. 1990. "From Rhetoric to Composition: The Teaching of Writing in America to 1900." In *A Short History of Writing Instruction*. Ed. J. J. Murphy. Davis, CA: Hermagorus.

Hardyck C. D., and L. F. Petrinovich. 1967. "The Functions of Subvocal Speech." *Project Literacy Reports*. Cornell University. (No. 8).

Hart, J. S. 1892. *A Manual of Composition and Rhetoric*. Philadelphia: Eldredge & Brother.

Hill, D. J. 1878. *The Elements of Rhetoric and Composition*. New York: Sheldon & Company.

Hashimoto, I. 1987. "Voice as Juice: Some Reservations About Evangelic Composition." *College Composition and Communication* 38: 70–80.

Heuscher, J. 1963. *A Psychiatric Study of Fairy Tales*. Springfield, IL: Thomas.

Irigaray, L. 1985. *This Sex Which Is Not One*. Trans. C. Porter. Ithaca, NY: Cornell University Press.

Irmscher, W. 1972. *The Holt Guide to English: A Contemporary Handbook of Rhetoric, Language and Literature*. New York: Holt, Rinehart and Winston, Inc.

Iser, W. 1978. *The Act of Reading: A Theory of Aesthetic Response*. Boston: The Johns Hopkins University Press.

Isocrates. 1966. *Isocrates, Book I*. Trans. G. Norlin. Cambridge, MA: Harvard University Press.

———. 1968. *Isocrates, Book III*. Trans. L. Van Hook. Cambridge, MA: Harvard University Press.

Jameson, F. 1981. *The Political Unconscious: Narrative as a Socially Symbolic Act*. Ithaca, NY: Cornell University Press.

Joyce, M. 1987. *afternoon, a story*. (Hypertext Fiction). Watertown, MA: Eastgate Systems.

Kane, T., and L. J. Peters. 1966. *A Practical Rhetoric of Expository Prose*. New York: Oxford University Press.

Kantor, K. 1974. "Creative Expression in the English Curriculum: An Historical Perspective." *Research in the Teaching of English* 9: 5–29.

Keep, C. and T. McLaughlin. 1995. "Yield." http://jefferson.village.virginia.edu/elab/hfl0279.html.

Kellogg, B. 1892. *A Text-Book on Rhetoric*. New York: Effingham, Maynard & Co.

Kitzhaber, A. R. 1953. *Rhetoric in American Colleges, 1850–1900*. Diss. University of Washington.

Kochman, T. 1981. *Black and White Styles in Conflict*. Chicago: University of Chicago Press.

Kolodny, A. 1975. "Dancing Through the Minefield: Some Observations on the Theory, Practice and Politics of a Feminist Literary Criticism. *Feminist Studies* 6.1: 1–25.

Kozma, A. 1966. "Getting with the Program: Women Tuning in to Computers Bit by Bit." *Chicago Tribune*, 3 Nov., Section 13: 3.

Kress, G. and T. van Leeuwen. 1996. *Reading Images: The Grammer of a Visual Design*. London and New York. Routledge.

Kyle, J. G. 1981. "Written Language in a Visual World." In *Exploring Speaking-Writing Relationships*. Eds. B. Kroll and R. J. Vann. Urbana, IL: NCTE.

Labov, W. 1984. *Sociolinguistic Patterns*. Philadelphia: University of Pennsylvania Press.

Lakoff, G., and M. Johnson. 1980. *Metaphors We Live By*. Chicago and London: University of Chicago Press.

Lakoff, R. 1982. "Some of My Favorite Writers are Literate: The Mingling of Oral and Literate Strategies in Written Communication." *Spoken and Written Language: Exploring Literacy and Orality*. Ed. D. Tannen. Norwood, NJ: Ablex.

Lawrence of Aquilegia. 1863. *Practiva sive usus dictaminis*. Ed. L. Rockinger. *Briefsteller und Formelbucher des eilften bis vierzehnten Jahrhunderts*. Munich.

Leggo, C. 1991. "Questions I Need To Ask before I Advise My Students To Write in Their Own Voices." *Rhetoric Review* 10.1: 143–152.

Liberman, A. M., F. Cooper, D. Shankweiler, and M. Studdert-Kennedy. 1967. "Perception of the Speech Code." *Psychological Review* 74: 431–459.

Lunsford, A., and L. Ede. 1990. *Singular Texts/Plural Authors: Perspectives on Collaborative Learning*. Carbondale: Southern Illinois University Press.

Macrorie, K. [1968] 1985. *Telling Writing*. 4th Ed. Upper Montclair, NJ: Boynton/Cook.

Mallon, T. 1989. *Stolen Words: Forays into the Origins and Ravages of Plagiarisms*. New York: Ticknor and Fields.

Mandelbaum, K. 1987. *Recipient-Driven Storytelling in Conversation*. Ph.D. Diss., University of Texas.

Markley, R. 1988. *Two-Edg'd Weapons*. Oxford, UK: Clarendon Press.

McCarthy, M. 1965. Interviewed by E. Niebuhr. In *Writers At Work: The Paris Review Interviews, 2nd Series*. New York: Viking.

McGuigan, F. J. 1973. "Electrical Measurement of Covert Processes." In *The Psychophysiology of Thinking*. Ed. F. J. McGuigan. New York: Academic Press.

Miller, S. 1989. *Rescuing the Subject: A Critical Introduction to Rhetoric and the Writer*. Carbondale: Southern Illinois University Press.

Moffett, H. Y., and W. H. Johnson. 1937. *Basic Writing: A Textbook for College Freshmen*. New York: Harper & Brothers.

Moi, T. 1985. *Sexual/Textual Politics*. London and New York: Routledge.

Moulthrop, S. 1991. *Victory Garden*. (Hypertext Fiction). Watertown, MA: Eastgate Systems.

Mulderig, G., and L. Elsbree. 1990. *The Heath Handbook*. 12th Ed. Lexington, MA: D.C. Heath.

Murphy, J. J. 1974. *Rhetoric in the Middle Ages: A History of Rhetorical Theory from Saint Augustine to the Renaissance*. Berkeley and Los Angeles: University of California Press.

————, ed. 1971. *Three Medieval Rhetorical Arts.* Berkeley and Los Angeles: University of California Press.

Murray, D. 1985. *A Writer Teaches Writing.* Boston: Houghton Mifflin.

Newcomer, A. G. 1893. *A Practical Course in English Composition.* Boston: Ginn & Co.

Ong, W. 1982. *Literacy and Orality: The Technologizing of the Word.* New York and London: Methuen.

Perrin, P. 1939. *An Index to English.* Chicago: Scott, Foresman and Company.

Phelps, L. W. 1988. *Composition as a Human Science.* New York: Oxford University Press.

Piaget, J. 1926. *The Language and Thought of the Child.* New York: Harcourt Brace.

————. 1928. "Logique génétique et sociologique." *Etudes Sociologiques.* Geneva: Librairie Droux. (Reprinted from *Revue Philosophique de la France et de l'Etranger* 53: 161–205.)

Plant, S. 1995. "Babes in the Net." *New Statesmen & Society* 8.337 (Jan. 27): 28.

————. 1996. Interview by Matthew Fuller. *Intelligence Is No Longer on the Side of Power.* http://193.170.192.5/meme/symp/contrib/sadie.html. 2 April.

————. 1995. "Net Gains: Academic Journals and Networks in the United Kingdom." *New Statesmen & Society* 8.337 (Jan. 27): 39–40.

Plato. 1961. *The Collected Dialogues of Plato.* Eds. E. Hamilton and H. Cairns. Princeton, NJ: Bollingen Series LXXI, Princeton University Press.

Poulet, G. 1980. "Criticism and the Experience of Interiority." In *Reader-Response Criticism: From Formalism to Post-Structuralism.* Ed. J. P. Tompkins. Baltimore: The Johns Hopkins University Press.

Quigley, S. P., and P. V. Paul. 1984. *Language and Deafness.* San Diego, CA: College-Hill Press.

Quintilian. 1987. *On the Teaching of Speaking and Writing: Translations from Books One, Two and Ten of the* Institutio oratoria. ed. J. J. Murphy. Carbondale: Southern Illinois University Press.

Reagon, B. J. 1995. "African American Oral Traditions." Talk presented at the annual convention of the Conference on College Composition and Communication, Washington, D.C. 23 March.

————. 1994. "Still on the Journey" (Sound recording review). *Down Beat* 61.1: 14.

Reed, A., and B. Kellogg. 1894. *Higher Lessons in English: A Work on English Grammar and Composition.* New York: Maynard, Merrill & Co.

Ritchie, J. 1989. "Beginning Writers: Diverse Voices and Individual Identity." *College Composition and Communication* 40.2: 152–174.

Roark, A. 1991. "Bettelheim Plagiarized Book Ideas, Scholar Says." *Los Angeles Times.* Feb. 7. Front Page, A28.

Russell, D. 1990. *Colorworks 1: The Red Book.* Cincinnati, OH: North Light Books.

————. 1990. *Colorworks 2: The Blue Book.* Cincinnati, OH: North Light Books.

————. 1990. *Colorworks 3: The Yellow Book.* Cincinnati, OH: North Light Books.

Safire, W. 1992. "The Take on Voice." *New York Times Magazine* 28 June: 14.

Scholes, R. 1985. *Textual Power.* New Haven: Yale University Press.

Scollin, R., and S. B. K. Scollin. 1981. *Narrative, Literacy, and Face in Interethnic Communication.* Norwood, NY: Ablex.

Sheridan, T. [1762] 1968. *A Course of Lectures on Elocution.* Menston, UK: Scholar Press.

Showalter, E. 1985. "Feminist Criticism in the Wilderness." *The New Feminist Criticism.* Ed. E. Showalter. New York: Pantheon.

Smith, F. 1988. *Understanding Reading.* Hillsdale, NJ: Lawrence Erlbaum.

Sokolov, A. N. 1972. *Inner Speech and Thought.* Trans. G. T. Onischenko. New York: Plenum Press.

Solomon, R. C. 1994. "Recapturing Personal Identity." *Self As Person in Asian Theory and Practice.* Eds. R. T. Ames with W. Dissanayake and T. P. Kasulis. Albany: State University of New York Press.

Sterne, L. 1980. *Tristram Shandy.* New York: W.W. Norton.

Stevens, K. N. 1960. "Toward a Model for Speech Recognition." *Journal of the Acoustical Society* 32: 47–55.

Stevens, K. N., and A. S. House. 1972. "Speech Perception." *Foundations of Modern Auditory Theory,* Vol. 2. Ed. J. V. Tobias. New York: Academic Press.

Stewart, D. 1972. *The Authentic Voice: A Pre-Writing Approach to Student Writing.* Dubuque, IA: Wm. C. Brown.

————. 1990. "The Nineteenth Century." *The Present State of Scholarship in Historical and Contemporary Rhetoric.* Ed. W. B. Horner. Columbia and London: University of Missouri Press.

Stewart, Mrs. D. (Patricia). 1995. Letter to author, 27 November.

Stoehr, T. 1968. "Tone and Voice." *College English* 30.2: 150–161.

Taylor, I., and M. M. Taylor. 1983. *The Psychology of Reading.* New York: Academic Press.

Trilling, L. 1972. *Sincerity and Authenticity.* Cambridge, MA: Harvard University Press.

Trudgill, P. 1974. *The Social Differentiation of English in Norwich.* Cambridge, UK: Cambridge University Press.

Volosinov, V. N. 1973. *Marxism and the Philosophy of Language.* Trans. L. Matejka and I. R. Titunik. Cambridge, MA: Harvard University Press.

————. 1987. "Reported Speech." *Readings in Russian Poetics: Formalist and Structuralist Views.* Ed. L. Matejka and K. Pomorska. Ann Arbor, MI: Michigan Slavic Publications.

Vygosky, L. S. 1986. *Thought and Language.* Ed. A. Kozulin. Cambridge, MA: MIT Press.

Watt, W. W. 1952. *An American Rhetoric.* New York: Rinehart & Co.

Webster, N. 1789. *Dissertations on the English Language.* Boston: I. Thomas.

Welty, E. [1937] 1965. *One Writer's Beginnings*. New York: Warner Books.

Wertsch, J. V. 1985, *Vygotsky and the Social Formation of Mind*. Cambridge, MA: Harvard University Press.

Whitman, W. 1982. *Complete Poetry and Collected Prose*. Ed. J. Kaplan. New York: The Library of America.

Williams, J. [1981] 1990. *Style: Toward Clarity and Grace*. Chicago: University of Chicago Press.

Williams, J. D. 1983. "Covert Language Behavior During Writing." *Research in the Teaching of English* 17.4: 301–312.

Woodmansee, M., and P. Jaszi. 1994. *The Construction of Authorship: Textual Appropriation in Law and Literature*. Durham and London: Duke University Press.

Wordsworth, W. 1967. "Preface to the Edition of 1815." In *English Romantic Poets*. Ed. D. Perkins. New York: Harcourt, Brace & World.

Zoellner, R. 1969. "Talk-Write: A Behavioral Pedagogy for Composition." *College English* 30.4: 267–320.